The Identity of Man

By the same author

The Mesolithic Age in Britain
The Mesolithic Settlement of Northern Europe
Archaeology and Society
Prehistoric England
From Savagery to Civilization
Prehistoric Europe: the economic basis
Excavations at Star Carr
The Study of Prehistory
World Prehistory: an outline
Prehistoric Societies (with Stuart Piggott)
The Stone Age Hunters
World Prehistory: a new outline
Aspects of Prehistory
Star Carr: a case study in Bioarchaeology
The Earlier Stone Age Settlement of Scandinavia
World Prehistory in New Perspective
Sir Mortimer and Indian Archaeology
World Prehistory and Natural Science
Mesolithic Prelude

Grahame Clark

The Identity of Man
as seen by
an archaeologist

Ellen Machama

Methuen & Co. Ltd

First published in 1983 by
Methuen & Co. Ltd
11 New Fetter Lane, London EC4P 4EE

First published as a
University Paperback in 1986

Photoset by
Rowland Phototypesetting Ltd,
Bury St Edmunds, Suffolk
Printed in Great Britain at the
University Press, Cambridge

British Library Cataloguing in Publication Data
Clark, Grahame
 The identity of man: as seen by
 an archaeologist.
 1. Ethnopsychology
 I. Title
 155.8   GN 502

 ISBN 0-416-33560-8

To Hugo de Balsham, Bishop of Ely (1257–86)

Contents

Illustrations

Acknowledgements

I would like first to acknowledge my wife's patience over yet another book and her valuable help in removing some of its imperfections.

I am indebted to the editors of the *Annual Review of Anthropology* for allowing me to incorporate (pages 154–8) certain passages from my essay on 'Archaeology and human diversity' contributed to the 1979 volume (pages 1–20). It was the invitation to contribute this essay that served as a catalyst for the present book, though it should be made clear that the topic chosen for my essay was entirely my own.

Illustrations

A number of the illustrations used in this book were contributed by individuals and museums, to each of whom I am most grateful:

Mrs J. Marshall, figure 13
The Trustees of the British Museum, figures 24, 26, 31, 35, 42, 45, 50 and 52
The Peabody Museum of Archaeology and Ethnology, Harvard, figure 27
The National Museum, Copenhagen, figure 28
The Dominion Museum, Wellington, NZ, figure 35
Dr I. E. S. Edwards, figures 38, 40
Pierre de Manasce Collection, figure 48
Museum of Fine Arts, Boston Mass., figures 53, 54
Calouste Gulbenkian Foundation, Lisbon, figure 55

Other illustrations are taken from the following published works which are duly acknowledged:

Figures 1, 2, 15: Bernard Campbell, *Human Evolution*, figures 5:12, 7:11 and 9:7 (London 1967)
Figures 3, 4: Sir William Le Gros Clark, *The Fossil Evidence for Human Evolution*, figures 13 and 14; 4 and 1 (Chicago 1964)
Figures 5, 17: Grahame Clark, *Archaeology and Society* (3rd edn), figures 50 and 25 (London 1957)
Figure 6: O. N. Bader, *Quartar*, bd. 18, Taf. XXVII
Figures 7, 21, 22, 46: Grahame Clark, *World Prehistory* (3rd edn), figures 39, 38, 222 and 34 (Cambridge 1977)
Figures 8, 9: Desmond Morris, *The Biology of Art*, pl. 17 and figure Y1 (London 1962)

Figure 10: Nancy K. Sandars, *Prehistoric Art in Europe*, figure Y.2 (London 1968)

Figure 11: H.-G. Bandi et al., *The Art of the Stone Age*, front., (London 1961)

Figure 12: S. L. Washburn and P. Dolhinow (ed.), *Perspectives on Human Evolution*, figure 1:9 (New York 1972)

Figure 14: Richard G. Klein, *Proc. Prehist. Soc.* XXXV p. 85 (1969)

Figure 16: Ole Worm, *Museum Wormianum*, front. (Amsterdam 1655)

Figure 18: John Wymer, *Lower Palaeolithic Archaeology in Britain*, figure 28, no. 40 and figure 82, no. 218 (London 1968); A. J. Arkell, *The Old Stone Age in the Anglo-Egyptian Sudan*, p. II no. 3 and pl. 25, left (Khartoum, 1949); H. D. Sankalia, *Prehistory and Protohistory of India and Pakistan*, figure 28 (Bombay 1962)

Figure 19: Grahame Clark in *Origins of Civilization* (ed. P. R. S. Morey), figure 1 (Oxford 1979)

Figure 20: I. G. Pidoplicko, *Late Palaeolithic Dwellings of Mammoth Bones in the Ukraine*, figure 42 (Kiev 1969)

Figure 23: Demetrios R. Theocharis, *Neolithic Greece*, pl. IV, VI, VIII and IX (Athens 1973)

Figure 25: John Brailsford, *Early Celtic Masterpieces from Britain in the British Museum*, figure 91 (London 1975)

Figure 29: F. Boas, *The Central Eskimo*, figure 492 (Washington 1888)

Figure 30: W. W. Fitzhugh, *Environmental Archaeology and Cultural Systems in Hamilton Inlet, Labrador*, figure 22 (Washington 1972)

Figure 32: Ellen Anderson, *Folkedragter i Nationalmuseet*, pp. 52, 55 and 61 (Copenhagen 1961)

Figure 33: W. Fagg, Tribes and Forms in African Art (London 1965)

Figure 37: Adolf H. Schultz, *The Life of Primates*, figure 57 (London 1969)

Figure 38: Grahame Clark, *Aspects of Prehistory*, figure 14 (Berkeley 1970)

Figure 40: I. Woldering, *The Art of the Pharoahs*, pl. 9 (London 1963)

Figure 44: *JNES* 39 (1980) p. 21, no. 4

Figure 49: Jessica Rawson, *Ancient China. Art and Archaeology*, figure 36 (London 1980)

Figure 50: Maz Loehr, *Ritual Vessels of Bronze-Age China*, cat. no. 38 (New York 1968)

Figure 54: M. L. Gothein, *A History of Garden Art*, vol. II, figure 442

Figure 56: *Historical Relics unearthed in New China*, figure 95 (Peking 1972)

Preface

One reason why I have dedicated this book to the founder of my college is that I believe a college to exemplify supremely well one of my main themes. A college operates over the centuries by feeding successive generations with the values embodied in a common history. It is true enough that the values transmitted by particular institutions derive in large measure from the circumambient culture and even to a degree from mankind at large. The fact remains that not even the most universal values can be apprehended except in the idioms of particular cultures and institutions. Another and more personal reason is the opportunity it gives to acknowledge the extent of my obligation to Hugo's foundation. I can never forget that Peterhouse enabled me to embark on prehistoric research by electing me Hugo de Balsham Research Student or that it subsequently bridged the gap between achieving a research degree and obtaining a junior teaching post in the university by appointing me Bye-Fellow of the college and giving me the leisure needed to write my first books.

Half a century ago it was no easy matter for an undergraduate to acquire the academic background for a career in prehistoric archaeology. Yet on balance I was more fortunate than I realized to escape the more specialized courses in archaeology now on offer in many universities. At that time prehistoric archaeology rated for only one part of a Cambridge Tripos and even so was taken as part of a comprehensive course in anthropology. This led to exposure to two major and in some respects complementary disciplines. To begin with it involved specializing in my old school subject history, but doing so in the ambience of a society renowned for the quality of its historical scholarship. Although to a certain extent involuntary, this apprenticeship in history stood me in good stead. It meant that when I came to archaeology I did so not as a distinct discipline so much as a way of extracting historical information about the past from its material detritus. In this way I was set on a path that led among other things to *World Prehistory* in its successive and expanding editions.

For an aspiring prehistorian a comprehensive exposure to anthropology was no less invaluable. Physical Anthropology and Human Palaeontology brought home the duration of the evolutionary process and the sheer length of prehistory. Comparative Ethnology served to emphasize that archaeological artefacts were designed to serve purposive roles as well as providing media for classification. Above all, Social Anthropology – and the classic monographs of Radcliffe Brown and Bronislaw Malinowski were still relatively warm from the press when I read the Archaeological and Anthropological Tripos – highlighted the social role of artefacts and emphasized the imperative need to interpret archaeological data in terms of social systems. It is small wonder that I should have entitled my first general book *Archaeology and Society* or that I should have made a point in my inaugural lecture at Cambridge, 'The study of prehistory' (1954), of distinguishing between the kind of history based to some degree on written documents and thus able to take cognizance of individual persons, and prehistory which in default of documents was only able to resolve the past in social terms.

Anthropology by its nature invites the task of defining man, the basic unit of the study. On the other hand definition can be a taxing process, something undertaken as a rule only to meet a specific contingency. Such a one arose from an invitation to deliver the Hitchcock Foundation lectures to a general academic audience at the University of California, Berkeley, in 1969. In the opening lecture of the series published under the title *Aspects of Prehistory* I broached a theme central to those treated in my present book by insisting that

Human values, and by definition behaviour conditioned by these values, cannot be 'natural' . . . ; they can only be artificial, the product not merely of human society but of the history of particular human societies.

An opportunity to develop this line of thought was offered ten years later by another invitation from California, this time to contribute the opening essay on a topic of my choice to the *Annual Review of Anthropology* issued from Stanford University. Under the title 'Archaeology and human diversity' I suggested that cultural diversity based on the growth of distinct traditions underlay the entire process of humanization. In this respect the behaviour of men developed in marked contrast with that of animals conditioned much more completely by the genetic codings of the several species. Whereas biological inheritance made for homogeneity of behavioural patterns within breeding populations, the distinctive historical heritage of different traditional societies made for an increasing diversity of behaviour among the various societies of men. From there I went on to suggest that another and in some ways more potent source of cultural enrichment stemmed from the differentiation of roles within societies. Hierarchy and social inequality were seen as key factors in the intensification of culture that has marked the more advanced societies in the course of the last 5000 years. Here, again, I was only giving expression to a point of view nourished by long practice as an archaeologist. In stressing the importance of social factors in prehistory in the course of my Cambridge inaugural I went out of my way to comment:

> After all, if we had remained in a state of primitive communism, we would still be bashing one flint against another and living lives nasty, brutish and short. We can agree with our Soviet colleagues that civilization has ever been a product of class society.

The present book, written during my first year of retirement from Peterhouse, is offered not as an *ex cathedra* pronouncement but as a summary reflection on a topic that has engaged my attention throughout my life as a professional archaeologist with a special concern for prehistory. The task of an archaeologist and not least of a prehistoric archaeologist is one of incessant if absorbing toil. His sources are not to be found in archives or libraries. They have first to be laboriously recovered from the ground and then subjected to ever more intensive scrutiny by an increasingly complex range of scientific and technical procedures, not to mention sensitive but rigorous stylistic analysis, before the process of historical interpretation can even begin. For many archaeologists the excitement of discovery in the field, coupled with the interest of directing new techniques to the recovery, dating and analysis of finds, compensate so amply that too many of them fail to ensure adequate publication of their findings, an increasingly heavy chore but ultimately the only justification for archaeological activity in the field. For those concerned above all with synthesis and the quest for meaning, the pursuit of archaeology finds its keenest reward in the insights it is capable of giving into the nature of man. The main impulse behind this book is the conviction that archaeology and anthropology between them are capable from their new and wide perspective of throwing a unique light on the identity of man.

Grahame Clark
Cambridge   23 September 1981

1
Introduction

The new knowledge of prehistory . . . has now so developed that it must change our thoughts about ourselves. It must change our attitude towards the so-called 'humane' studies, it must change our outlook on history, it must, in fact, change our whole philosophy.

CHARLES SINGER (1932)[1]

This book is offered in the belief that men and the powers they acknowledge as divine are the true measure of the world. It was written at a time when humane studies are often dismissed as élitist, escapist and a threat to the material well-being of the common man and indeed when man himself is sometimes reduced in the popular imagination to an incidental, if not accidental by-product of cosmic or even biochemical processes. Distaste for contemporary consumer societies based on the almost universal assumption that the cure for our ills lies in the more effective production and the more equal distribution of material goods and services from a limited and in some cases diminishing stock of natural resources is understandable, but, unless as a spur to action, pointless. Nostalgia for the past is futile as a posture and dangerous if used to fuel merely reactionary attitudes to forces as overwhelmingly powerful as those which have so rapidly transformed traditional into modern industrial societies. For a more positive approach to the future we need above all a contemporary sense of what it means to be human. Only so can we define the values we need to sustain if we are to retain our status as human beings, a status acquired by our largely prehistoric forebears in the course of many thousands of generations. From the perspective opened up by archaeology and its associated disciplines our problem is not how to engulf or process more materials or even how to divide them into more equal portions. It is, rather, how to maintain in the face of mounting threats a quality of life unique to our own species.

Before the rise of archaeology as a discipline in the course of the last three centuries, European man gained his principal insight into what it meant to be human in part through his own intuitions but to a significant degree through teaching based on the written word. The barbarian successors of the Roman Empire were civilized by Christian teaching and by pagan literature salvaged from the ancient world. Yet although the written word (and its oral counterpart) was crucially important it was by no means the only source of Gothic and Byzantine civilization. Rediscovery of the Classical World was stimulated and nourished to an outstanding degree by material manifestations in the form of architecture, sculpture, gems, coins and ceramics. The drive to identify with the material embodiments of antiquity was one of the principal sources of connoisseurship and in due course of archaeology. Similarly the Christian church sought to convey its message through architecture, wall paintings, sculpture, church ornaments, vestments, stained glass, mosaics and not least the illumination of manuscripts, as well as through the word. Indeed the medieval church had no real alternative seeing that it had to proselytize and minister to congregations few if any of whose members could read. Preaching and reading of the scriptures needed to be supplemented by iconography, structures and material objects embodying doctrine and symbolizing the faith.

If documentary sources remain even less sufficient for historical purposes today, this is for quite the opposite reason. It is not that men in general are unable to read, but that so restricted a part of human history, as this is becoming known to us today, is recorded in words. The last 300 years have seen as big an explosion in history as in the natural sciences. While the world has shrunk to the point at which we can hardly remain insensible of the local if not parochial nature of our recorded histories, it has at the same time expanded temporally to such a degree that even the longest spans of history recorded in words are insignificant by comparison with those embodied in the material artefacts recovered by archaeology. The advance of prehistoric archaeology in step with the earth sciences and biology has indeed given men pause to ponder the meaning of their humanity, while at the same time transforming the perspective from which they view not merely their past, but their present and their future. Furthermore the application of archaeology to the many literate civilizations of historical times, including our own, has completed the task of bringing into one sphere of discourse the cultural achievements of all mankind.

Archaeology has traditionally engaged a wide variety of appetites and emotions as well as many and sometimes highly specialized intellectual concerns. This is not the only or indeed the main reason for the strength of its appeal. At first glance it might seem excessive to claim that archaeology excites for what it can tell us about humanity and our own individual lives. Is it not the case that, in the absence of the human actors who have vanished from prehistory and appear only fitfully on the stage of history, archaeologists have to depend on the rubbish and ruined structures of communities long perished? It is true enough and something we do well to remember that no individuals survive from prehistory. Indeed, unless he is confronted with signed artefacts or the burials of named persons like Egyptian pharaohs or Christian kings or prelates, the archaeologist even when dealing with historic periods has to make do with social entities rather than individuals. It is an ineluctable fact that few indeed of the countless legions of the dead are known to us by name even for fully historical periods. The converse is no less true that all human beings, known to us by name or totally unknown, acquired their humanity by virtue of belonging to social groups and sharing common histories. Men are not born with culture. They acquire it from their fellows. There is a very direct sense in which the artefacts handled by archaeologists are more than material objects: they are very embodiments of humanity.

Yet, if from this point of view archaeology can only address us as men or as members of particular communities, from another it can speak to us directly as individual persons. It is after all a unique feature of man and one shared at differing levels of intensity by every individual in his right mind that he is aware of his context in past, present and future time and is capable of asking questions and reasoning from the answers. All of us can respond in some measure to the challenge issued half a century ago by the eminent historian of technology, Charles Singer, quoted at the head of this chapter.

The point is worth emphasizing that archaeology and its associated disciplines have advanced our knowledge of prehistory at an accelerating rate since Dr Singer offered this comment. What was prescient in 1932 is now so evidently well-founded as to call insistently for an answer.

From certain points of view the advances which have made it possible to define the place of man in the natural order and trace the course of his unwritten history during the last two or three million years must rank among the outstanding achievements of our age. Archaeology is now appreciated and pursued not just in Europe and the United States but in all parts of the world.[2] Furthermore it is a striking circumstance that although supplemented overseas by the most advanced industrial nations, now including Japan and the USSR, the burden of archaeological research has been willingly assumed by many of the newly independent states with pressing claims on their resources – so precious is the sense of identity in territories whose pre-colonial past is in so many cases almost entirely prehistoric. From whatever motives archaeological research has in the last fifty years spread over the remaining territories of the globe and at the same time has encompassed the entire temporal range since the first emergence of the genus *Homo*. Since Charles Singer's lecture it has become progressively more possible to conceive of a genuine world prehistory as a setting for the several histories of the diverse civilizations of men. Thanks in large measure to intensive and long-sustained investigation of the Lower and Middle Pleistocene deposits of Africa and most notably of Olduvai Gorge we now have fossil documentation for the emergence of successive forms of man and his earliest essays in technology. Exploration and increasingly detailed programmes of excavation over extensive territories in northern and eastern Eurasia have thrown significant light on the expansion of *Homo sapiens* during the Upper Pleistocene, including surprisingly early colonization of the circumpolar territories of the USSR and the initial occupation of Japan. Despite some recent interruption, impressive advances have been made in tracing the origin and early history of the specifically Chinese focus of human culture. Again, the indigenous scholars of India and Pakistan have gone far to transforming the prehistory of their sub-continent, as well as defining some of the key problems for future research. At the same time archaeologists are busy unveiling unexpectedly precocious prehistoric cultures in mainland southeast Asia antecedent to the age of polities and monumental structures. Radiocarbon dating more than anything has been responsible for showing that Australia was colonized by man far earlier than anthropologists had ever imagined as well as promising to date successive stages in its prehistory. Radiocarbon dating has also served to pinpoint the much later processes of occupying the Pacific islands, colonizing successive zones of the New World and documenting the early history of agriculture. In summary, we are far better informed than Charles Singer could have been on such vital topics as the emergence of successive types of man, the spread of *Homo sapiens* over new territories and the evolution in many areas of new modes of subsistence as the basis for the emergence of more complex hierarchical societies.[3]

If our knowledge of the unwritten phases of human history is deeper and more exact, as well as more extensive than was the case fifty years ago, this has been brought about in large measure through a more effective partnership between archaeologists and natural scientists.[4] This is particularly apparent in respect of dating, an area that has grown in importance as exploration extended into territories beyond the remotest reach of historical chronologies. The greatest advances have been made by measuring the radioactivity remaining in materials whose half-life, the time taken for half the residual radioactivity to decay, has been established by physicists. The most convenient method used so far is radiocarbon dating since this can be effected from organic substances commonly present on archaeological sites, including charcoal, food-refuse or artefacts made from materials like antler, bone or wood. The drawback to radiocarbon is that its half-life is relatively short. This means that the age of samples can only be determined within an acceptable range of probability over the period of hardly more than 70,000 years. In practice indeed it is only for the latter half of this range that radiocarbon dates are of much real use to the prehistorian. Even so the method provides a system of relative dating of world-wide application for a period of crucial importance in human history. Within five years of the publication of the first lists of age determinations a string of laboratories was established in western Europe and the United States of America with outliers in the Antipodes and Japan. At the same time the international organ *Radiocarbon* was set up to publish the results. By 1970 radiocarbon dating laboratories were active throughout the world community of science.

Parallel work went forward in the development of potassium-argon dating. Although not so readily applied to archaeological deposits, its much longer half-life meant that potassium-argon was capable of yielding dates over an enormously longer range. It is mainly due to potassium-argon determinations of volcanic rocks from long stratigraphical sequences exposed in Africa, notably in Olduvai Gorge, in the Lake Rudolph region and in the Omo sequence of Ethiopia, that the biological and cultural evolution of early man during the Early and Middle phases of the Pleistocene can be set in temporal perspective. The massive contribution of natural science to the basic chronology of prehistory is only part of the story. As the literature[5] shows very clearly an extensive range of the earth sciences, biology, chemistry and physics, as well as science-based technology in many fields have been brought to bear on problems raised in archaeological research to the benefit of all concerned.

No less important than the harnessing of natural science to the reconnaissance, recovery and analysis of archaeological data, has been a notable change of attitude on the part of archaeologists towards social studies.[6] Although the task of recovering, dating and classifying artefacts continues to claim much of the time of a working archaeologist, there has been a marked increase of interest in the communities responsible for them. Archaeological evidence is increasingly being interpreted as a source of information about economic and social systems and the changes these have undergone. This has affected archaeology in a number of ways. Among other things it has influenced priorities in research and the methods used in pursuing it. It has also radically affected the constituency of archaeology. This is no longer seen as the exclusive preserve of connoisseurs, museum men or scholars, but as a field of concern to a wider community and not least to individuals. Although the notion that archaeology was at once about ancient society and a matter of concern to contemporary society was advertised in *Archaeology and Society* as long ago as 1939, it is only in recent years that it has had much impact on professional archaeologists. Not surprisingly it has made most headway in environments where prehistoric archaeology is pursued in the same institutions as anthropoloy or where, as in the United States, it so often forms part of the discipline of cultural anthropology.[7] Unquestionably the new trend has been favoured by the development of computer technology which has so greatly eased the task of extracting economic and social information previously hidden in the embarrassing wealth of often discrete data thrown up by archaeological excavation.[8] One need only cite the wealth of social information to emerge from multivariate analysis of prehistoric cemeteries containing large numbers of burials with grave goods.[9] Fifty years ago archaeologists would have been content to describe, classify and date grave goods and then probably only from the richer graves. Today they seek to extract information from every grave, preferably from complete cemeteries, bearing on such matters as differences in status between age, sex and class groups, not to mention wide areas of demography and palaeopathology. Enough has been said to underline the fact that our knowledge of the unwritten history of mankind has widened and deepened in all manner of ways, in part through improvements in archaeological technique and in part by closer and more intelligent co-operation with a wide range of natural sciences and fields of social study. Our information has improved beyond measure at the very time that the findings of archaeology have come to be accepted as a matter of concern to anyone who spares a thought for the meaning as well as the business of life.

The question which above all others has engaged the attention of philosophers and teachers as well as plain men through the ages is the basic one of identity. What does it mean to be a man? Or, to frame it in more contemporary terms, what does it mean to be a man rather than any other form of Primate? The question does not cease to be asked even when the teachings of so many venerable religions tend to be dismissed as fables and philosophers have in the main ceased to address themselves to the concerns of lay men and women. Nor does natural science any longer confront the admiring and expectant community it once did. Apart from loss of public faith in the inevitable beneficence of scientific discovery, the reductionist outlook associated with science is to say the least unhelpful. However useful and indeed valid it may be for laboratory purposes to describe a human being in terms of his chemical constituents comprised in a formula or even at a higher level as an organization of sentient protoplasm, it is worse than useless to a person in quest of his identity. Let it be said that wide-ranging reductionist explanations emanate less from practising scientists accustomed to employ them legitimately to further limited ends in the course of their own professional work than from those who seek to popularize science or use it to lend credibility to their opinions. It is significant that some of the more extreme proponents are to be found in the ranks of advocates of the philosophical rights of animals. When the application of reductionism to the moral universe can lead a writer of Peter Singer's standing to doubt whether the life of a man is inherently more valuable than that of a mouse,[10] most human beings will be species-prejudiced enough to seek elsewhere for enlightenment about their own condition. Conversely it is hardly surprising that the most convincing exposures of the misuse of reductionist explanations stem from scientists accustomed to their legitimate use. If W. H. Thorpe is cited specifically, this is because as an eminent ethologist concerned with observing and explaining animal behaviour his views are of particular relevance to beings who, though aspiring to a kind of divinity, still remain animals by nature. Thorpe's attitude is well summed up in his observation that: 'a highly complex organ, or system, has capacities and potentialities that are the properties of the system and not merely of the components of the system.'[11] What is true of an organ must apply even more to an organism and what goes for an amoeba must apply still more to a jellyfish, a grasshopper or a man. As Thorpe expressed it so well, the key lies in the principle of hierarchy: 'Science can in fact pass beyond reductionism just because its reality is hierarchically arranged.' It is the chief aim of the present book to suggest that the identity of man is to be sought above all in his history as this has become known through the exploration of prehistory. From the perspective already available to us the evolution of man and his culture embodies a kind of hierarchy in time.

Archaeology, in partnership at one extremity with animal ethology and palaeontology and at the other with recorded history, backed throughout by a galaxy of natural sciences and a variety of social studies, has already revealed at least in outline how certain Primates made themselves into men. Beyond that it has shown how men, while remaining animals by nature, have entered, at least potentially, on a new dimension of life shaped increasingly by patterns of behaviour transmitted through social groups conforming to specific cultures. At the same time we do well to heed and bear constantly in mind a wise pronouncement of Kenneth E. Boulding that: 'All we know of the past, whether in cosmology, palaeontology or human history is the record of it.'[12] The only record that runs through the whole of history is that embodied in the structures and other artefacts shaped by countless generations of men all of whom were until comparatively recently preliterate. In this respect at least archaeologists can rejoice in the tangible, testable, pervasive and constantly increasing nature of their documentation. Few jibes are wider of the mark than that which designates archaeologists as men who overlook *Homo sapiens* in their preoccupation with *Homo faber*. It is precisely in the works of their hands that successive forms of men have left the most eloquent memorials of their evolution as social beings. Artefacts form the only continuous documentation of the achievements of successive stages in the development of man. The archaeological record extends from his appearance down to modern times and in doing so reveals the cultural values of human communities over the whole span of their evolution. Above all it monitors the process of humanization by which men have distanced themselves from the non-human Primates. Throughout by far the greater part of his history man's cultural capital remained pitifully small, changed extremely slowly over immense ranges of time and displayed only a minor degree of diversity as between one group and another. Acceleration in the rate of change accompanied by a perceptible increase in cultural diversity first appeared in conjunction with *Homo sapiens* in the latter part of the Upper Pleistocene. The process of cultural enrichment and diversity was to reach a series of climaxes in the several civilizations that developed in different parts of the world during the last 5000 years, many of them leaving behind at least traces of historical records. The diversity of cultural expression encountered by anthropologists as they studied people until only recently living outside the modern industrial economy was hardly less marked.

One of the dilemmas of post-industrial societies, as yet only partially perceived, is how to reconcile the homogenizing tendencies of a world increasingly organized on the basis of machine technology, rationality and natural science with the diversity of human values which epitomize the history of men. The threats posed by modern industrial society to the physical environment of mankind are widely appreciated both intellectually and at the level of daily experience. The dangers posed to humanity itself are too often ignored at least by the intelligentsia. Where they are recognized this is mainly at a popular level in the form of apprehension and indignation at the cultural impoverishment and loss of identity suffered too often in the name of progress. Yet if the impoverishment of the world's genetic bank accomplished by the progressive extinction of animal and plant species threatens our economic well-being, the homogenization of human culture challenges our very identity as men.

2
Men and Primates in fossils and in life

Without men, no culture, certainly; but equally, and more significantly, without culture, no men.

CLIFFORD GEERTZ[1]

A basic assumption of this book is that a sense of identity lies at the root of human personality. To ask what it means to be human is to pose a question men have asked themselves through the ages. Until quite recently their main, indeed the only, reinforcement of their own intuitions was the web of allegories, speculations, riddles or revelations conveyed in such media as legend, drama, poetry or sacred formulae and texts. One of the main things Charles Singer had in mind when he spoke of the need to adjust to prehistory was precisely that it and human palaeontology in particular was capable of providing objective evidence in place of conjecture for answering the key question of identity in an idiom acceptable to current thought. Since Darwin, Huxley and Lyell brought man firmly within the scope of the evolutionary process, it has become possible for the first time to pose questions about our origins with some prospect of obtaining answers capable of being tested by verifiable evidence. In a word we are now in a position to examine positive, tangible data bearing on our identity as men. Archaeology even permits us to evaluate manifestations and trends of the present day and judge the extent to which they are likely to enrich, impede or threaten the future of our species.

Once the hypothesis that man has emerged as an organism in the course of evolution is accepted, it follows that one way of defining his identity is to consider his status in the context of his fellow Primates. This can be done in terms of behaviour as well as of morphology. Since these fall into the spheres of distinct disciplines, ethology in the former and anatomy and palaeontology in the latter, there is a case for considering them separately. On the other hand it is important to lay some emphasis on their interaction: form and function go together. Another thing to remember is that, if taxonomic classification is to enhance understanding as well as to provide labels, close attention needs to be paid to fossils illustrating the evolutionary process. The phylogenetic factor should always be remembered in considering problems of taxonomy.

The evidence of fossils[2]

Although the fossil evidence bearing on human origins is immensely richer than it was in Huxley's day, it remains exceedingly incomplete. Attempts to devise phylogenetic classifications of man, his ancestors and closest relatives are, and look like remaining for some time, provisional. Even so we are on safe ground if we assign ourselves to the Primate order and within this even a visit to the zoo should be enough to convince us that we stand closest to the anthropoid apes. Among the many close similarities between ourselves and the great apes noted by Sir William Le Gros Clark were those relating to muscular anatomy, the structure and disposition of the visceral organs, chromosome patterns, blood groups and metabolic processes. Furthermore it is of particular interest that he should have described the human brain, the very engine of man's ultimate dominance, as 'little more than a magnified model of the brain of an anthropoid ape'. Le Gros Clark also went out of his way on the other hand to draw attention to differences between men and anthropoid apes. Of these, the ratio of brain to body weight, dentition and limb proportions are of outstanding evolutionary significance. Yet it remains true that as Huxley contended in 1863: 'the structural differences which separate man from the gorilla and the chimpanzees are not so great as those which separate the gorilla from the lower apes.'[3] If the taxonomic

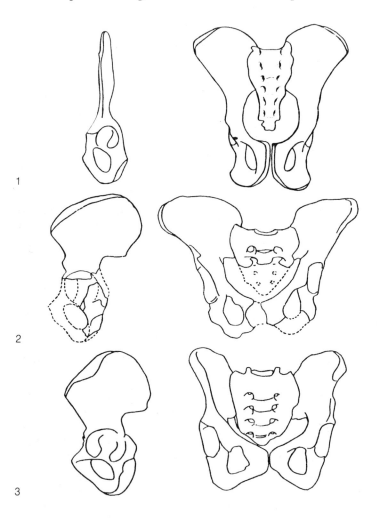

Figure 1 The evolution of the pelvis. 1 *Chimpanzee.*
2 *Australopithecus africanus.* 3 *Homo sapiens sapiens* (Bushman).

differences between men and the anthropoid apes are no greater than those existing between other mammals accepted as phylogentically close, it seems right to class them both as members of a single superfamily, the Hominoidea. The differences between them may be expressed by assigning them to distinct families, the Hominidiae to accommodate men and closely related forms and the Pongidae for the existing anthropoid apes and their fossil relatives.

The most significant anatomical differences between the hominids as a whole and the anthropoid apes relate to posture and gait reflected among other ways in the form of the pelvis (Figure 1). The increased size of the brain was a relatively late development in the history of the hominids. In respect of posture and gait hominids and pongids diverged in opposite directions from the generalized Primate condition. Whereas the former assumed an upright position and habitually progressed on two feet, the latter underwent progressive modifications, including a lengthening and a more powerful muscular development of the arms, in a direction pointing to arboreal brachiation as a normal way of getting about. This divergence was linked with other significant differences. For instance the substantial freeing of the forelimbs from locomotion implied that among the hominids the hands were freed for operations formerly carried out to a large extent by the teeth. This in turn resulted in a reduction in the size and prominence of the canines and a lightening of the jaw. The adoption of an erect posture also meant that the head could be balanced rather than suspended from the vertical column. This in turn reduced the need for such powerful muscular attachments to the cranium and so facilitated the enlargement of the brain that more than anything was to mark the physical evolution of man (Figure 2). Another outcome of standing and moving upright was to diminish the importance of the sense of smell by comparison with that of vision. This, together with the freeing of the hands and the development of the brain, was closely associated with the manufacture and manipulation of artefacts.

Le Gros Clark's insistence on the priority of an upright stance over the marked expansion of the brain in the history of hominid evolution finds strong support in the appearance in the fossil record of *Australopithecus*, a genus of the hominid family having an upright posture but still endowed with a brain well below the size of that attributed to man. During the initial phase of their discovery the new fossils were liberally endowed with Latin names indicative of species or even genera. Today the consensus inclines against recognizing any distinct genera in this group. Instead the fossils are divided into two species, *Australopithecus robustus* having a heavy jaw set with relatively large

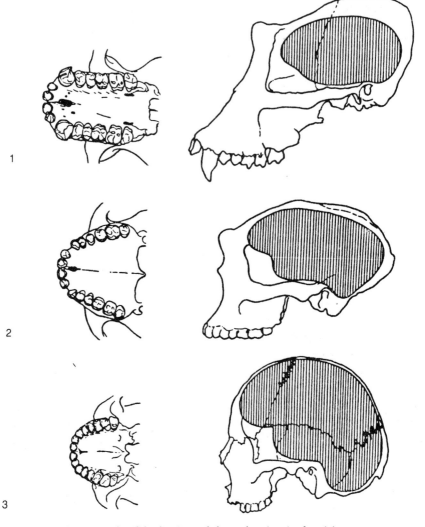

Figure 2 The growth of the brain and the reduction in dentition among certain primates. 1 Gorilla. 2 *Homo erectus*. 3 *Homo sapiens sapiens*.

and broad molars and premolars and only small, narrow canines and incisors, and *A. africanus* with a lighter jaw and teeth of more human character (Figure 3). If the extensive milling surfaces of the *A. robustus* molars and premolars and the relative atrophy of the incisors and canines point to a specialized herbivorous diet, perhaps with an emphasis on chewing nuts and hard roots, this would make it easier to understand how two such distinct, though closely allied forms could have shared the same terrain, since the dentition of *A. africanus* argues for an omnivorous diet. Again, it would seem to follow that *A. robustus* diverged from the main line of development through specialization very much as the pongids had done at an earlier stage.

Table 1 Simplified taxonomy of the family Hominidae.

Families	Genera	Species	subspecies
Hominidae	*Homo*	*H. sapiens*	*sapiens* *neanderthalensis* *steinheimensis* *soloensis* *rhodesiensis*
		H. erectus	*africanus* *heidelbergensis* *javanensis* *pekinensis*
		H. habilis?	
Pongidae	*Australopithecus*	*A. africanus*	
		A. robustus	

Without question the future lay with the more omnivorous group to which *A. africanus* belonged. Its very dynamism, by contrast with the robust group, coupled with insufficiencies of the fossil record, has

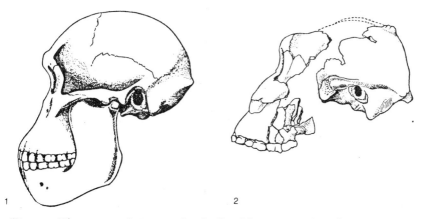

Figure 3 The contrast between the skulls of the two species of Australopithecus. 1 *Australopithecus africanus.* 2 *Australopithecus robustus.*

greatly complicated the task of reconstructing the course of hominid evolution. This became clear as soon as Louis Leakey began to classify the hominid fossils recovered from successive beds of the Pleistocene exposures in the Olduvai Gorge, Tanzania. When, for example, he attributed certain fossils to the genus *Homo* and classified them as *H. habilis*, due to an assumed ability to fabricate and use stone tools, professional anatomists were often more inclined to attribute them to *A. africanus*. It is a tribute to Le Gros Clark's perspicacity that he should have appreciated from an early stage that the decision whether or not to attribute the new fossils to the genus *Homo* would have to depend in the final resort on behavioural characteristics, and in particular on whether the animal to which they related could speak or fabricate tools,[4] rather than on morphological niceties. Whether the hominids represented by particular fossils were or were not able to engage in articulate speech is something we would indeed like to know. In respect of tool-making the record is ample so far as flint and stone artefacts are concerned. Unfortunately it is not always easy to interpret. The mere recovery of artefacts from the same deposits as hominid fossils does not of itself tell us for certain who made them. Whether the hominids fabricated the tools or whether they were victims of more evolved forms which did is often a question.

Early controversy over *Homo habilis* has long since been placed in a new perspective by a flow of relatively well-dated fossils[5] from Olduvai, as well as from the Koobi Fora Formation and the Karari plateau of east Rudolf and the Omo sequence of southwest Ethiopia. From these, taken together, a much fuller, though still incomplete, picture is beginning to emerge of the course of hominid evolution in east Africa during the Lower Pleistocene. It is now established that the robust group of Australopithecines persisted well into the Pleistocene without undergoing perceptible morphological change until they finally succumbed about a million years ago, presumably in competition with more effective species. By contrast there was a dramatic quickening in the evolution of other hominids in the course of the Pleistocene. Whether and how far the more gracile group of Australopithecines contributed directly to the main line of evolution is still not certainly determined and is not in any case a matter of great moment. What the new discoveries have shown beyond reasonable doubt is that hominids of the genus *Homo* had certainly emerged between 2 and 3 million years ago. The lower part of the Koobi Fora Formation yielded the almost complete cranium of the genus *Homo*, having a cranial capacity of *c.* 775 cc, dating from perhaps 3 million years ago. Furthermore lithic industries of Oldowan character, comprising chopper-like implements and numerous flake tools, have been re-covered from the KBS tuff in the same formation dating to *c.* 2.6 million. Other early occurrences of this type of industry include those in the Shungura Formation of the Omo sequence of Ethiopia from *c.* 1.9 to 2 million and from Bed 1 at Olduvai dating from *c.* 1.9 million years ago.

If the immensely long Lower Pleistocene witnessed the as yet shadowy appearance of *Homo* the tool-maker, the fuller records of the Middle and Upper Pleistocene make it possible to visualize more clearly the evolution both physical and cultural of progressively more advanced groups. The first to come into reasonably sharp focus is *Homo erectus* whose fossils are already known from east and north Africa, Europe, Indonesia and China. As their name suggests members of this group, while short in stature, probably not exceeding 5 feet, stood and moved in an upright posture. Their brains, on the other hand, while larger than those of their predecessors, were still small by comparison with later members of the genus. The average cranial capacities of the better-preserved fossils from Java and north China were of the order of 860 and 1000 cc respectively. Their flat-topped skulls had receding foreheads and continued to be attached by power-ful neck muscles. Their jaws, set with large teeth of human type, were heavy and chinless and were matched by massive and continuous bone ridges above the eye-sockets. The face was prognathous, projecting markedly below the nose which was broad and flat. Although *Homo erectus* is uncouth to contemplate even in fossil form – so much so that he was once classed as a distinct genus – the fact remains that he made a number of significant advances in adapting to his environment. As the distribution of his fossils shows, he had advanced beyond the warm territories occupied by the Australopithecines and early members of the genus *Homo*. In the west he spread as far north as the Rhineland and Hungary and in the east as far as the Peking region on the northern margin of the great plain of China. He also made notable advances in respect of technology. In both east and north Africa he had enriched the repertoire of stone industries by adding the manufacture of bifacially flaked hand-axes to the Oldowan base. In north China, where he continued to make do with flakes and choppers, he was certainly using and presumably making fire, an important require-ment for cave-dwelling in those latitudes. The evidence of the animal bones from his occupation levels shows that he was outstandingly successful as a hunter. Although he obtained some two-thirds of his meat in the form of venison, he also took elephant, rhinoceros, water buffalo, horse, camel, bison, antelope and sheep, not to mention such formidable competitors as sabre-toothed tiger, cave bear, leopard and hyena.

The Upper Pleistocene witnessed a dramatic acceleration in the tempo of human evolution. The evidence for this is of two distinct though, as I shall hope to show, causally connected kinds. The most marked feature on the palaeontological side was the multiplication of fossils attributed by general consensus to our own species. By comparison with *Homo erectus* the fossils of *Homo sapiens*, which to judge from the skull bones from the Thames gravels at Swanscombe,[6] began to appear during the final interglacial phase of the Middle Pleistocene, was marked above all by enlargement of the brain and reduction in the size of dentition. The forehead was now rounded rather than receding, brow-ridges although still in some cases prominent no longer formed a continuous ridge or torus, mastoid processes were now prominent and pyramidal in shape, the teeth were smaller, the jaw lighter and a definite chin was present for the first time (Figure 4). Within this general definition there was scope for considerable variation and this was especially marked between fossils dating from before and after *c.* 35,000 years ago. Among the earlier fossils a number of distinct

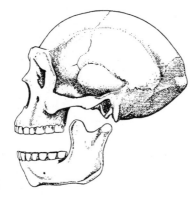

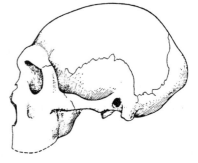

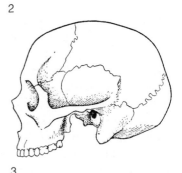

Figure 4 Skulls of three species of man. 1 *Homo erectus pekinensis.*
2 *Homo sapiens neanderthalensis.* 3 *Homo sapiens sapiens.*

subspecies of *Homo sapiens* may be recognized. The earliest, that represented by fossils from Swanscombe and the German locality of Steinheim, had brains of a size well within the range of modern man, respectively *c.* 1325 and 1100 cc in capacity. Minor differences in fossils from South Africa and Indonesia have similarly been recognized at subspecific level. Much the largest group, named collectively after the fossil discovered at Neanderthal as long ago as 1856, itself displays a wide range of variation.[7] The aberrant features of a group from western Europe, including a large facial area and powerful brow-ridges, have been accounted for as the outcome of isolation in an extreme periglacial environment. It is interesting to note that despite his reputation as a very model of 'primitive man', men of the western group of Neanderthals in fact possessed an unusually large brain (*c.* 1425 cc av.). The fact that both in Europe and southwest Asia Neanderthalers were so often directly followed by the skeletal remains of men of fully modern appearance may well have served to exaggerate the contrast between them in the public mind. It is now commonly accepted that the differences have been overdone and the distinction can be adequately marked at subspecific level by designating the younger group as *H. sapiens sapiens*. Another conclusion almost universally accepted today is that all existing races of men belong to this particular subspecies.

Accelerated change is also apparent at this time in the behavioural sphere. Since skeletal remains of early man have so often been recovered, not least in the form of burials, from stratified deposits containing archaeological material, it has been recognized that palaeontological and cultural change were closely synchronized. The commonest stratigraphical link between the two sequences is that provided by flint and stone industries since traces of these survive most often and most abundantly. The conjunction between the appearance of the first representatives of the genus *Homo* and the primitive Oldowan lithic industry has already been noted, as have the advances effected by *Homo erectus*. The first sapient men represented, notably by the fossils of *H. sapiens steinheimensis* from Swanscombe, are identified with the culminating point of hand-axe technology and the production of some of the finest lithic artefacts ever made. Among his successors Neanderthal man was responsible for a transformation in lithic technology sufficiently marked over parts of Europe, north Africa and southwest, central and northern Asia to attract the designation Middle Palaeolithic. Although certain groups continued to make hand-axes, the main emphasis shifted to flake tools struck from prepared cores, an innovation that economized both labour and raw materials as well as promoting a greater variety of products and styles. Neanderthal man was also responsible for a further northward extension of human settlement reaching almost to the Arctic Circle in European Russia. In adapting to colder climates he constructed substantial artificial dwellings which to judge from their plans were almost certainly covered by skins stretched over poles and made taut by weights disposed round their perimeters.

During the closing stages of the Pleistocene men of *Homo sapiens sapiens* type made further advances along much the same lines. As research expanded from western to central and eastern Europe, to north Africa and over parts of southwest Asia, it has become more than ever apparent that even within this limited area Upper Palaeolithic industrial assemblages displayed a much greater variety of forms, techniques and styles and a notable increase in the tempo of cultural change. At the same time full advantage was taken of geographical circumstances to expand further the range of human settlement. The low sea-levels that prevailed while extensive ice-sheets remained permitted movement from southeast Asia over Indonesia and ultimately by quite short sea passages to Australia and again from mainland China and Korea to Japan. Other opportunities were seized when ice-sheets contracted and divided, as they did in north America. When a passage opened between the Cordilleran and Laurentide ice-sheets the Paleoindians passed through it to reach the Atlantic coast, traverse Mesoamerica and establish themselves on Magellan Strait, all within a few thousand years. It goes without saying that in adapting to new environments in the course of his expansion modern man continued the process of innovation and diversification already apparent during earlier phases of his expansion.

If ancient man grew in biological effectiveness by elaborating his technology and extending his range of settlement, he displayed his advance as a human being above all in the growth of his imagination and his capacity to visualize himself, his fellows and the animals which shared his environment. It is true that this aspect of his development is more sparsely documented in the archaeological record and even more difficult to interpret than evidence for subsistence or technology. The most informative sources include evidence for treatment of the dead, ornamentation of the person and the representational and symbolic art by which he sought to establish an emotional rapport with the generative forces of wild animals.

Although as yet we have no evidence that *Homo erectus* accorded careful burial to his dead there are signs that he at any rate ceased to treat them with mere indifference in the manner of the anthropoid apes. In particular it has been observed that many of the skulls from Choukoutien had been treated in a manner known from at least one Neanderthal skull and from recent skulls from Melanesia:[8] the *foramen magnum*, the hole at the base by which the spinal cord joined the brain, had been artificially enlarged as if to facilitate, as in the case of Melanesian skulls, the extraction of the brain. The possibility that we have here evidence for ritual cannibalism on the part of *Homo erectus* has to be borne in mind. On the other hand there is certain and abundant evidence that sapient men, even those of Neanderthal type, were already practising carefully ordered burial of their dead: indeed at the Mughâret es-Skhūl, Mount Carmel, a cemetery of at least ten burials was found suggesting the practice of regular burial as a normal rite (Figure 5). The burial practices of modern man show evidence of notable elaboration. Already in Upper Palaeolithic contexts observation of the disposition of ornaments makes it evident that the dead were buried in their clothing adorned with their personal finery and as a rule sprinkled with red ochre and occasionally accompanied by implements and weapons. Few discoveries exemplify Upper Paleolithic burial ritual more aptly than the graves of people of *Homo sapiens sapiens* type recently excavated by Soviet prehistorians at Sungir, Vladimir, not far east of Moscow (Figure 6).[9] In addition to the thousands of perforated beads sewn or threaded onto headgear, body garments and leggings, the dead were provided with mammoth-ivory bracelets, small animal carvings, flint tools and, in one case, a set

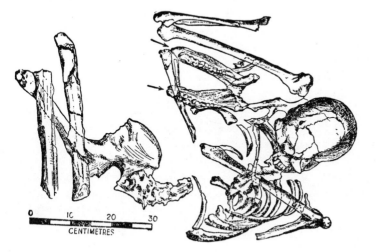

Figure 5 Burial of Neanderthal man in the Mughâret es-Skhūl, Palestine, accompanied by the mandible of a very large pig (after T.D. McCowan).

Figure 6 Burial of Upper Palaeolithic man with personal finery, Sungir, USSR.

of magnificent ivory spears. Recognition of the implications of death, including the need to separate the dead from the living and provide for their future well-being, were thus already well established during the late Pleistocene. In future ages burial rituals were to take on forms which, more especially in hierarchically structured societies, were to assume ever more extravagant guises. Human necrology as revealed by archaeology is a standing testimony to the insufficiency of any narrowly economic interpretation of the human experience.

The wealth of ornaments placed with burials even during the Old Stone Age is enlightening from another point of view. It reflects the significance attached to individuals as persons and above all as players of roles in structured communities. Although for all we know Neanderthal man may have decked himself and his associates with all manner of garlands, feathers or other perishable substances, it remains true that up to the present not a single perforated bead or other ornament has been recovered with his remains, despite the number of burials excavated and carefully recorded. When ornaments first appeared in Upper Palaeolithic contexts they did so in abundance and in a great variety of forms and styles (Figure 7). Although in most cases made from substances ready to hand, such as animal teeth, ivory, stone pebbles or mollusc shells, in some instances materials had been imported from a distance through the medium of social interchange, from sources in some cases beyond the range of seasonal movement. Numerically beads were the commonest form, but bracelets and

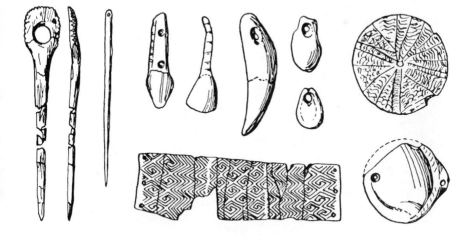

Figure 7 Personal ornaments made by Upper Palaeolithic man in eastern and western Europe.

pendants of varying kinds were by no means rare. Although most beads were left plain, bracelets and pendants were more often ornamented in a variety of patterns by incision or drilled pits. Like funerary rites personal ornaments offered wide scope for elaboration and diversity, serving to denote and emphasize group identity and social status.

The first people to design personal ornaments were also the origin-ators of the graphic arts. We have seen that they applied decorative designs to the ornaments. The converse is also true that they some-times wore small works of art as ornaments, as testified by the stylized female figurines carved from coal and designed as units of a necklace from the cave of Petersfels, south Germany. Whatever purpose the artists had in mind when they sculpted, engraved or painted the walls and ceilings of their caves and rock-shelters, we can only speculate. What is beyond dispute is that their work betokens areas of awareness and sensibility for which there is no comparable evidence from earlier phases of hominid evolution. In this connection it is worth recalling the experiments on apes and more particularly on chimpanzees summarized by Desmond Morris (Figures 8 and 9)[10]. Although he tells us that the animals found the use of pencils on paper and painting by means of their fingers self-rewarding and enjoyable, it seems abun-dantly evident that they had nothing of substance to say. Congo, the

Figure 8 The Chimpanzee Congo choosing a colour for painting.

star performer of the London zoo, turned out fan-like patterns, but Morris had to conclude that

> no ape, no matter how old or experienced, has yet been able to develop graphically to the pictorial stage of simple representation. The study of the birth and growth of imagery must therefore be made with human infants rather than apes.

The aesthetic impulse was, as Herbert Read once pointed out, a necessary outcome of evolving consciousness. Just as in the case of the individual the development of intelligence was matched by a sense of harmony and integration calling for aesthetic satisfaction, so it might be supposed was it the case in the evolution of *Homo sapiens*. The creation of works of art, like the devising and wearing of personal ornaments, was a self-rewarding and, according to W.M.S. Russell, a therapeutic activity for men who had passed a certain threshold of awareness. And the same applied to the fashioning of other artefacts. The evolution of the flint or stone hand-axe in the course of the Middle Pleistocene at the hands of *Homo erectus* and the earliest sapient men exemplifies a profound truth, resoundingly confirmed through the rest of time, that craftsmen derive satisfaction and stimulus in shaping materials into artefacts, not only economically and efficiently, but in a manner that is aesthetically gratifying.

Figure 9 The development of drawing with age on the part of a young chimpanzee (1, 3) and a young boy (2, 4).

The iconography of Upper Palaeolithic art reflects the common preoccupations of its makers. The human figure that predominated in three-dimensional sculpture and in reliefs, but played only a minor role in the engravings and paintings of the cave art of western Europe, centred above all on the image of the fecund female (Figure 10). Similarly the animals depicted on the cave walls in a manner that betokens the keenest direct observation (Figure 11) played a central role not merely in the food quest but in the very lives of the Upper Palaeolithic hunters, for whom, apart only from other human beings, they were by far the most important element in the total environment. It remains to mention the recent revelation that under high optical magnification an intricate though still elusive system of notation can be seen to have been engraved on the surfaces of antler and bone artefacts.[11] Although it still awaits definitive interpretation this notation, in which it is perhaps not too fanciful to see a forerunner of writing and mathematical signs, should serve to remind us of the intellectual, as well as the economic, technical and asethetic capabilities of the earliest men of completely modern type.

Even the most summary overview of the course of human evolution should be enough to underscore a broad synchronism between its biological and cultural aspects. It must be accepted that the emergence of specifically human behaviour implied major modifications in primate morphology. No creatures requiring all their limbs for locomotion would be able to develop the manufacture and use of tools

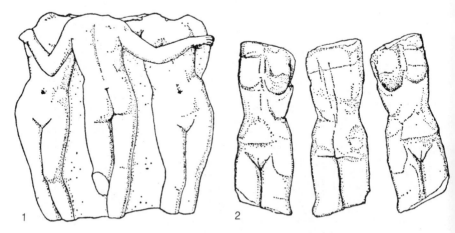

Figure 10 The female form in art. 1 Late Classical relief of the Three Graces. 2 Three views of an Upper Palaeolithic figurine carved from haematite, Ostrava-Petřkovice, Czechoslovakia.

Figure 11 Animals painted by Upper Palaeolithic man on the rock surface at Lascaux, France.

as a prime means of adapting to and exploiting their environment. Similarly the way of life of *Homo erectus*, let alone of any more advanced type of man, called for a substantially more developed nervous system including a more capacious brain than that found among the Australopithecines and still more among the anthropoid apes. Again, it would hardly have been possible to engage in articulate speech without significant modifications of the vocal anatomy found in the non-human primates. This is far from claiming that the emergence of culture as a factor in determining behavioural patterns had to wait on the autonomous progress of biological evolution. The outstanding speed-up in the rate of primate evolution that occurred in the case of the genus *Homo*, by contrast for example with the apparent lack of change on the part of *Australopithecus robustus* once this had appeared fully formed in the fossil record, points to the introduction of some distinctive dynamic factor. The most likely agency is culture itself. The pronounced advantages conferred on an organism by the ability to make tools to standard patterns must have favoured genetic mutations which in any way facilitated this ability. As Washburn pointed out, once a Primate had started to use tools:

> then selection would favour shorter fingers and larger thumbs. The use of tools would change the direction of evolution and the form of

the hands. . . . Our hand is the result of at least half a million years of tool use.[12]

Other outcomes of the selective pressures exercised by the use of increasingly effective tools, something which began a good deal earlier than Washburn could have known when he wrote, include a number reflected in the fossil record. These embrace a reduction in the size of the anterior teeth, the doubling, even trebling of brain capacity and a marked increase in the area of the cortex associated with the hand by contrast with a stabilization or even a slight reduction in that associated with the foot. The fact that the earlier stages in the development of tools proceeded in such close conjunction with the biological evolution of man the tool maker as an organism may help to account for the extreme slowness with which cultural development unfolded through the long ages of the Lower Pleistocene. By contrast, once the basic biological adjustments to culture had been effected, cultural change was able to speed up at an increasingly rapid pace. The subspecies *H. sapiens sapiens* seems not to have changed physically, apart from the effects of such factors as diet and the control of disease, since he emerged some 30,000 to 35,000 years ago. During this time the tempo of cultural change was no longer restrained by the process of biological adjustment. The rate of development was henceforward determined by social factors, as Bernard Campbell has so convincingly argued.[13] In the course of prehistory man made himself as well as the type of society we term human.

The evidence of ethology[14]

An alternative way of defining human identity is to compare man's behaviour with that of his nearest living relatives. Before doing so a word may be in place concerning common descent. Our survey of the fossil evidence should have been enough to emphasize the extreme remoteness of the relationship between man and even his closest living relatives. It was after all around 30 million years ago that the hominid and pongid stems diverged in the course of evolution. On the other hand, however remote, the anatomical and physiological evidence for physical kinship between men and other primates, not to mention lower forms of life, is as we have seen unambiguous. The presumption must surely be that the basic appetites of men derive from the same source as their bodily structures. Although this presumption provides one of the main driving forces of ethological research, it has met with a more selective response from laymen. Thinkers wedded to the idea that man can be perfected by tinkering with his institutions have as a rule preferred the dreams and speculations of Rousseau and the philosophers to the science of Darwin and Huxley. To such, man's animal heredity is something to be overlooked or dismissed as irrelevant to the onward march of progress. At the other extreme, purveyors of reductionist natural science have achieved fame and profit by feeding the less educated with what may well have appeared to the grateful multitude as a licence endorsed by the leading figures of Victorian science to wallow in permissive animality. The position adopted in the present book rests on the double premise that man's animal ancestry has to be accepted with all its implications but that through the process of humanization documented in the course of prehistory his animal nature can be tamed or at least directed into different channels by a process of nurture and when necessary by constraint. Our animal origins should be enough to warn us against accepting the eighteenth-century notion, which still ensnares some well-intentioned people into believing that man is by nature good and has only been corrupted by civilization. The tenor of this book will be to argue that the contrary is nearer the truth.

The remoteness of the relationship between man and the other Primates has not lessened the interest shown by ethologists in the behaviour of apes and monkeys. Attention was at first focused on animals readily accessible in zoos. It was the suggestiveness of these studies pioneered by Solly (now Lord) Zuckerman,[15] tempered by doubts about the validity of research on captive animals, that led Jane Goodall and others to engage in the long-term observation of apes and monkeys in their wild habitats. The most significant outcome of these studies from our point of view has been to show that in certain respects Primates and most notably chimpanzees display aptitudes and tendencies that bring them close to the threshold of culture. At the same time it seems important to enter a *caveat* against the use of the term 'pre-adaptive' to describe aspects of modern Primate behaviour: the animals to whom such a term might appropriately have been given have been fossilized these 30 million years. The factual observations made by ethologists in the field of Primate behaviour remain of the utmost interest to anyone concerned with the emergence and definition of specifically human modes of behaviour. To an archaeologist, for whom the appearance of artefacts made to standard designs serves as a key marker, one of the most crucial questions to be asked of ethology is the extent to which Primates fabricate and use implements. A fact on which observers agree is the interest apes and monkeys display in handling and scrutinizing objects, an activity in which it is surely not fanciful to see one of the requisites for making and using tools. Animals of widely varying character have been observed utilizing objects already existing in nature to serve ends of their own, as when an Egyptian vulture throws a stone in its beak to open an ostrich egg or a California sea-otter scoops up a stone with one arm to break an abalone mussel shell brought up with the other. A more sophisticated procedure is followed by chimpanzees who use sticks or stems to poke termites from their nests and convey them to their own mouths, since this involves some preparation including stripping foliage and breaking stems into convenient lengths. Even more suggestive is the way these animals have been observed to lengthen a stick to bring food within reach (Figure 12). The fact remains that the gap between chimpanzees and even the lowliest men in respect of tool using and even more of tool-making is immense. As W.H. Thorpe admitted in his masterly survey of the field:

> we are left with a tremendous chasm – intellectual, artistic, technical, linguistic, moral, ethical, scientific, and spiritual – between ape and man. And we have no clear idea as to how this gap was bridged.[16]

Figure 12 Chimpanzee fitting one bamboo cane into another so as to reach a bunch of bananas.

Archaeology can only begin to help for the 2 or 3 million years of which we have some records in the form of artefacts.

Another aspect of behaviour documented in the archaeological record and open to direct observation from ethnologists and ethologists centres on diet. By and large the dietary habits of chimpanzees in the wild have not been found to conflict in any fundamental way with the premise that a great divide in Primate evolution occurred when pongids concentrated more on vegetable foods and hominids on an omnivorous diet in which meat came to play a role of increasing importance. Ethologists have been keen to show on the other hand that while vegetarian in habit chimpanzees nevertheless relish meat when it comes their way and have even been seen on occasion suddenly to seize and devour young monkeys or small antelopes. The occasional nature of such episodes and the fact that they eventuated in sudden grabs on the other hand may be seen as at least as significant as the fact that they happened at all. Whereas among men hunting was an institution of basic importance not only for subsistence, but also in respect of technology and not least of social organization, among chimpanzees the accession of meat to diet was hardly more than an occasional episode.

A wide gap also exists in the disposition of food. Whereas individual apes and monkeys are expected to find food for themselves after weaning, the formalized sharing of food, something which has nothing to do with consumption of the kill in common by predators hunting in packs, is universal among the human societies observed by ethnologists. The rare occasions on which chimpanzees have been seen to engage even in casual food-sharing arose during episodes when animal carcasses happened to be available. This is suggestive in that as we know food-sharing was institutionalized in human society in the context of an omnivorous diet, which went in turn with a sexual division of labour in the quest for food (Figure 13). Women, because of the need to remain at or close to the home base in order to tend the young during their lengthy period of dependence, were effectively restricted to activities associated with foraging. Men on the other hand, being free to venture further from the home base, if necessary for lengthy periods, were adapted to engage in hunting. The contrast between the roles of the sexes was self-sustaining and even reinforcing. Every increase in cultural complexity magnified the need to educate the young, extended their period of dependence and reinforced the need to maintain the home base. Another factor worked in the same direction. The greater the contribution made by hunting, the greater the need to share. Whereas foraging was concentrated on

Figure 13 Sexual division of labour in the Bushman food-quest. 1 hunters off on an expedition. 2 woman and small child foraging close to home base.

readily accessible resources and was automatically shared among those participating in the quest, hunting was less predictable and when successful was liable to result in accessions of food too large for direct consumption. If a resource as valuable as meat was to be shared without dissension, the best way was to divide and distribute it according to accepted rules based on kinship. Among surviving hunter-foragers the distribution of meat on predetermined lines not merely avoids conflict, but makes for the physical and social viability of the group. Food-sharing was in each respect of adaptive advantage to societies of human character.

While the attraction between the sexes was doubtless paramount in determining social relations among animals, the more structured groupings involved in the kinship systems of human societies are no longer held to have originated primarily and certainly not exclusively in sexual requirements. It is true that as Zuckerman pointed out the Primates differed physiologically from other mammals in their capacity to mate during much of the menstrual cycle as well as at all seasons and that this may have favoured more prolonged heterosexual groupings. On the other hand field studies of chimpanzees have shown them to be outstandingly promiscuous in their mating habits. Schultz has emphasized another trend in the physiological evolution of the Primates, namely the extension of the life span and in particular of the infantile and juvenile periods during which the young were dependent for survival on parental care: whereas the period of dependence in the lemur is marginally less than 2½ years, in the macaque slightly over 6, in the gibbon between 8 and 9 and in the chimpanzee 11 years, in the case of modern man it is slightly over 20 years. The lengthening of dependence gave the young longer to acquire and practise the behavioural patterns needed for survival as adults. The size of the gap between man and chimpanzee in this respect calls for special remark. The most likely hypothesis is that it was the adoption of an increasingly cultural way of life which generated and sustained the selective pressures behind the rapid and marked extension of the period of dependency. The longer period of nurture certainly enhanced the prospects of survival by allowing more time for learning. The increased importance of the home base that went with a lengthening of dependence is documented in the archaeological record by traces of substantial dwellings built by Neanderthal man at Molodova in south Russia (Figure 14) which stand in marked contrast with the flimsy platforms set up nightly by chimpanzees. With established home bases went as we have seen economic partnership between the sexes, formalized food-sharing and the institution of the biological family group on an economic rather than merely sexual basis. The even more marked extension in the duration of adult life in the case of man is another artefact of the cultural way of life. Whereas among other Primates individuals barely outlived the reproductive period of the female, among men the post-reproductive phase of adult life commonly lasted as long as half the total life span. In purely biological

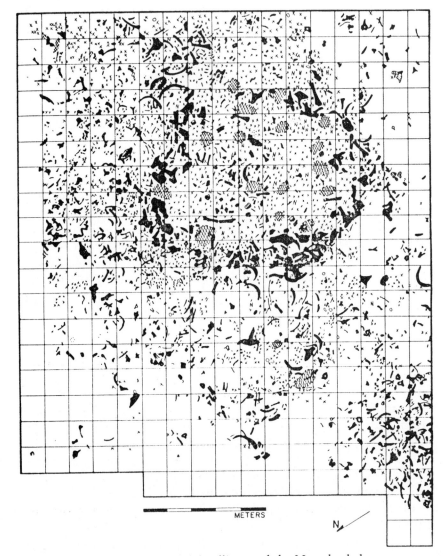

Figure 14 Traces of a substantial dwelling made by Neanderthal man, Molodova, Dnestr Valley, USSR.

terms life after breeding was brief because superfluous. An extension of life beyond only served as a useful function in terms of culture.

According to the zoologist Wynne-Edwards[17] the occurrence of some form of social integration in all animal populations is explained by the fact that it promoted survival by regulating dispersal. One of the mechanisms most widely encountered among birds and fish as well as among mammals is that of dominance hierarchy, according to which every individual stands in a definite relation to every other regarding access to food, territory and females (Figure 15). A key adaptive advantage of hierarchy is that it reduces the need for overt conflict, while at the same time ensuring a more economical use of resources. It remains highly eugenic in that it ensures preferential access to food and mates on the part of dominant individuals. Hierarchical systems, however contrived, are not only universal among men, but in some of their most structured forms have nurtured the most diverse and elaborate civlizations known to history or salvaged by archaeology.

As well as playing a key role in the genesis of civilizations, hierarchy in human society offered every individual a secure, if for most a humble place. The prototypes of preconditions for moral codes in the form of instinctive patterns of restraint were indeed deeply rooted in animal behaviour. When they were formulated as systems in human societies they reinforced and gave conventional directions to the

Figure 15 Ranking order displayed by a baboon troop moving across country. In the middle dominant males accompany females with infants. Two estrous females (hindquarters shown dark) are accompanied by adult male consorts. Below the centre juveniles and unattached adults precede and follow the heart of the group.

instinctive inhibitions that restrain aggression among animals and so made for survival. Among men, equipped with the progressively more effective weapons developed in the course of technological advance, the acceptance of moral systems became increasingly necessary for bare survival. Morality was also sustained by more positive forces. A regard for the rights and well-being of others and an emotional involvement in maintaining the values esteemed in different societies stemmed in all probability from the prolonged nurture of the young which as we have seen was such a marked feature of human societies. Moral systems owed their strength in the last resort to their adaptive value in making for the emergence and development of societies of human character. Because they were artefacts, moral systems and the methods used to enforce them were subject to wide variation and diversity. Indeed they soon became vital elements in the identities of individual cultures. The essential fact to remember is that, as Meyer Fortes has long insisted, human societies are invariably founded on rules, which served to define the limits within which instinct is allowed to operate and at the same time to reinforce the sense of identity of each particular culture.

Lévi-Strauss's shock pronouncement that the prohibition of incest is not merely a precondition for but in very fact constituted civilization was designed to underline the fact that human societies are not merely regulated by but are positively constituted by the observance of rules. The counterpart of incest taboo, the practice of exogamy, by which marriage partners had to be taken from outside the group, extended the area of social cohesion and rendered it more effective. The imposition of rules affected far more than mating arrangements. It made for better co-operation in the business of securing an adequate living, in disposing of the dead and in discharging the ritual obligations by which harmonious and fruitful relations were maintained with the ancestors and the other powers and forces that sustained the visible world. Another point to emphasize is that social rules are of their essence traditional rules. They are not part of any genetic inheritance, but acquired through incorporation by education, imitation and training in the ways of particular societies. To be effective rules need legitimacy and legitimacy is most effectively conferred by inheritance. The rules by which societies live are residues of their histories every bit as much as are their ancient monuments and their languages. This does not mean that social rules or traditions are static. Societies need to adapt if they are to survive when circumstances outside their control undergo change. Indeed, in their capacity to adapt sufficiently rapidly to survive human societies are greatly superior to organisms dependent on the slow process of biological change. Museums of paleontology are filled with the bones of animals dominant in their own day, but too specialized to adapt rapidly enough to environmental change to avoid extinction. The social traditions that engage the interest of historians and archaeologists have on the contrary managed to survive due to the much greater flexibility of the cultural mechanism.

Some form of communication is another necessity for all animals if for no other reason than that the very existence of species as breeding groups depends on the mutual recognition of potential mates. Human societies, which after all are constituted by sharing traditional patterns of behaviour, depend for their very existence on incomparably more sophisticated and precise modes of communication, notably articulate speech and, at a certain level of complexity, writing. Yet men continue to employ their senses in much the same way as other animals, although frequently supplementing their organs by artefacts. The use of smell or scent to proclaim identity, demarcate territory or express emotion, while of prime importance to many animals, only survives among men in a limited number of situations and it is significant that even in these it was commonly applied in artificial forms like deodorants or blended and purified perfumes. By contrast visual signs are more varied and richly developed among men than among other animals. When expressing emotion men are accustomed to employ their bodies in the guise of gestures, facial expression and to a limited extent even by changing colour. When it comes to signalling identity the human response is far more varied. Whereas animals are only concerned with biological attributes like age, sex or species, which can be perceived directly, men need to convey a much greater variety of identities and roles in the context of historically constituted and often highly structured societies. If men perceive the biological aspects of identity in much the same way as animals, for signalling the identity of social groups and the status and roles of individuals within their respective societies they make use in the main of artefacts. Some such signals are displayed on the person, notably in hair-dressing, make-up, body-painting, tatooing, clothing, ornaments and insignia of occupation or rank. Others are manifest in the production of almost every article used in daily life: pots and pans, baskets, bows and arrows, spears and axes are no mere receptacles or weapons, but symbols of cultural identity and hierarchy. And the same applies to larger structures such as dwellings, fortifications, temples or tombs. In short the whole apparatus of material culture has symbolic meaning and conveys signals over and beyond utilitarian function.

Auditory communication is of widespread importance for keeping individuals in touch with the group as well as attracting mates and warning intruders or rivals. Among non-human animals these basic needs are adequately met by using the limbs or vocal organs. Men also employ these elementary means for certain purposes, but characteristically they tend to supplement or even replace them by the use of a variety of instruments based on percussion, strings or wind. The special requirements of human societies on the other hand call for communication systems of another order, above all on those depending on articulate speech. Primatologists have recently applied themselves with ingenuity and persistence to testing the linguistic capacities of chimpanzees. Despite the most skilled tuition these animals can hardly be said to have proved themselves to be apt pupils. What is abundantly sure is that no chimpanzees encountered either in the wild or in zoos have been heard to engage in anything remotely comparable to articulate speech. This is hardly surprising. Wild animals do not make a habit of engaging in activities which serve no useful purpose. The question one is bound to ask is whether anthropoid apes have anything to talk about beyond the emotions and needs adequately signalled by emitting their customary calls and sounds? Among men on the contrary articulate speech serves needs so vital that even the most banal functions of human society could not be carried on, let alone transmitted to future generations without it. The habitual fabrication of tools to standard patterns and the conduct of social life according to rules determined by history rather than biology necessitated a mode of communication sufficiently flexible to take precise account of objects and persons as well as a variety of concepts relating to past and future as well as present time. Although not all human palaeontologists are prepared to infer articulate speech from fossil skulls, Bernard Campbell has argued that the lower posterior parietal area of the cortex, the most important of the areas of the brain associated with speech, underwent a marked development in the Middle Pleistocene, a period that as we have seen witnessed a rapid increase in the capacity of the brain and notable advances in the techniques of working flint and stone. Every advance in the complexity of social life enhanced the flexibility and precision of language, which was not only man's most important artefact, but in the most literal sense made possible the entire process of humanization. A further point should be emphasized. Men were not humanized by language in the abstract, but by the particular language spoken by members of their own communities. It is not for nothing that *The Shorter Oxford English Dictionary* defines a language as the 'whole body of words and of methods of combining them used by a nation, people or race' and speech as 'the form of utterance peculiar to a particular nation, people, or group of persons'. Language was at one and the same time a way of integrating social communities and of defining their separate identities *vis-à-vis* others. Some idea of the implications of this may be had by recalling that the Australian aborigines, who before the arrival of Europeans are thought to have numbered only a few hundred thousand, are reckoned to have spoken upwards of 500 languages and dialects. In the case of writing, both the script and the material of which the document was made were determined by culture. As well as conveying messages, inscriptions betrayed and indeed advertised the cultural identity of the scribe or at least of his master.

The crucial difference between animals and men rests in the respective importance of nature and nurture in the shaping of their behavioural patterns. Although ethologists have been able to detect certain preconditions of culture and have even, as in Thorpe's studies on bird song, been able to isolate patterns of learned behaviour shared by local populations, the fact remains that behavioural patterns among the lower animals are to an overwhelming extent innate, part of the genetic inheritance shared by members of the same species. Among men on the contrary genetic inheritance is overlaid by cultural patterns inherited by virtue of belonging to social groups constituted by sharing common histories. Whereas animal species were subject to substantially homogeneous and static behavioural patterns with individuals imprisoned in the present and effectively caged by their instincts, men are by comparison free. In the nature of things freedom is a relative concept. The prototypes and earliest versions of man only freed themselves over immense periods of time from total thralldom by creating and submitting to cultural patterns, and even today men of the most advanced culture are burdened as we know only too well by appetites which stem from far back in our animal ancestry. Certainly also the process by which man first achieved his humanity and individuals enter upon their inheritance involves costs as well as gains. In so far as men do achieve humanity they can only do so by submitting to a process akin to domestication. The survival of human societies depends in the short term on a substantial degree of compliance and conformity on the part of their members. Traditional codes are transmitted from the ancestors, incorporated in custom and rendered acceptable through religious beliefs and rituals. In the longer term on the other hand the situation is very different. The most notable feature of human societies is their capacity for adaptation and change. Whereas for example beavers go on and presumably have gone on for countless generations building their dams and birds and bees their nests, according to the unvarying and involuntary patterns derived like their bodily structures from their genetic heritage, archaeology and history reflect and indeed owe their very existence to the dynamic quality of human societies. The adaptability of animals is by no means negligible as we see from the ways in which they have accommodated themselves to life in cities. On the other hand the medium of culture has provided man with an incomparable ability to change and to diversify.

Before going forward in later chapters to review some of the ways in which men have diversified and enriched their social life, the question may well be asked how it is that human societies depending for their very existence on tradition and the observance of rules have nevertheless proved themselves as capable of change as history has shown them to have been. Paradoxically the answer lies in the freedom of individuals every one of whom owes his humanity to adhering to societies constituted by history. Men are free to the extent that they are able to imagine and engage in choices between objectives and alternative ways of achieving them. In a word they are free to the extent that they are capable of reasoning. The ability to reason, while it depends on the nervous system and the brain, can only be effective through the use of articulate language, by which alone it is possible to designate objects and their qualities, define and refine ideas and concepts, specify alternatives and judge correctly between them. It is thanks to language again that within the scope of historical awareness knowledge acquired by former generations can be accumulated and drawn upon at will. Men are able in this way to take critical stock of their existing situation and plan for the future in the light of the past. Again, thanks to the web of formalized social relations, including those arising from exogamy, men were constantly exposed to the stimulus of contact with different patterns of social life. When an archaeologist contemplates a section through the infill of a cave or the build-up of a settlement he is liable to see a number of complacent deposits the contents of each of which reflect a high degree of cultural conformity, separated by interfaces dividing one clearly defined cultur-al pattern from another. In some instances this may indicate no more than a break in the occupation of the site. In others the disconformity may reflect phases of rapid change when the cost of maintaining the status quo exceeded that of effecting a rapid transformation of the system as a whole. In seeking explanations it is right to look for underlying pressures, but if we may trust the evidence of history the immediate cause even of radical change is likely to have stemmed from the questioning of quite a small minority or even by a single individual. One should never forget that cultural patterns however firmly established are constantly subject to social selection according as they impede or promote the values of the group or prove adequate to withstand contingencies. The freedom of individuals to question social norms and press for change helps to explain why human societies were so much more successful than animal populations in accommodating themselves to changes in their environment.

A number of the attributes of greatest significance to man appear to be unique to societies of human character. Certain of these, including his attitude to the dead, to his own person, to other people and to other animals, have already been discussed in relation to the archaeological fossils illuminating the process of humanization. The remaining topic on which I ought to touch is that of human awareness. This is hardly the occasion, nor am I qualified to define consciousness in philosophical terms. What I have in mind is certainly more than the mere perception of messages relayed by the senses from the external world. My concern is rather with the faculty of being aware that one is conscious, not merely of objects or persons, but of qualities, of different dimensions of time and reality and not least of transcendent powers calling for worship. I am not interested here with the enrichment of personal life, vital as I recognize the role of individuals to be on societies of human type, but rather with the impact of certain areas of awareness on the cohesion and coherence of social communities. The impact of an appreciation of history on the identities of societies will be discussed in the next chapter. Here I would stress the role of religion as a system of belief and a procession of rituals in binding together and defining the identity of social groups. As in every other aspect or dimension of social life we are not confronted by religion in the abstract, but with specific religions shared by the individuals belonging to particular social entities. Religion is as much a badge of identity and in consequence an exemplar of diversity as any other aspect of human behaviour. It is not for nothing that the architecture, iconography and paraphernalia of religious practice have provided vehicles for some of the most extravagant and richly diverse manifestations of the multitudinous cultures of mankind.

3
Approaches to archaeology

Time, the great destroyer, is also the great preserver

HERBERT J. MULLER[1]

The fossil evidence for the emergence of man together with comparison between his behaviour and that of his nearest living relatives show
that men acquired and retain their status as human beings by conforming to cultural patterns. Men remain animals by appetite, as who may
doubt who considers how ostensibly civilized individuals behave
when for any reason the normal rules of society have been suspended.
It is only as animal drives are harnessed to the patterns and controls
shaped by human society that men are capable of entering fully upon
the comparatively recent dimension of life we recognize as human.
Since cultural patterns are by definition inherited by belonging to

groups constituted by historical experience rather than by genetic coding, it follows that to comprehend humanity fully we need to take account of the totality of human history. The only documents to survive from the whole range of history are the artefacts that embody the manifold traditions of mankind.

Attempts to reconstruct the course of man's cultural history have been made by thinkers having very different aims in mind. Those of basically humane outlook have been and remain concerned with history rather than generalities. They have always been preoccupied with identifying and exploring the distinctive traditions through which men have developed their characteristics as human beings. By contrast those of a more natural philosophical outlook have been more interested in defining the stages through which they conceived mankind to have passed in the course of evolution. They seek above all to define regularities and even laws in the development of human affairs comparable with those inferred by natural scientists. Although these concerns are complementary and often inform the outlook of the same individual, the history of archaeology shows that for long periods one or the other was predominant. The earliest archaeologists and antiquarians were concerned first and foremost with their cultural heritage and identity. The Age of Enlightenment ushered in a new era in which the main emphasis was natural philosophical and abstract. The dominant concern was then to trace what was conceived of as the progress of mankind. The last two or three generations have witnessed a marked reaction against scientism and an increasingly strong concern for humane values. Although making increasingly sophisticated use of natural science as a tool, most modern archaeologists see themselves as engaged in a historical study concerned with the emergence and development of the specific cultural traditions by and through which men have attained their status as human beings. This chapter reviews the three main phases in the history of archaeology: the antiquarian, the natural philosophical and the cultural historical.

Antiquarian

Early European antiquaries were preoccupied first and foremost with the sources of their own civilizations. Although the importance of the Classical world in this regard had been recognized long before the Renaissance as later defined by Burckardt, interest was certainly intensified in Italy during the fifteenth and north of the Alps during the sixteenth century. If scholars were mainly preoccupied with literature, the leaders of society at large responded more directly to the architecture, sculpture and minor arts of the Graeco-Roman world.

This was reflected in the eclipse of Gothic and the commissioning of works in the Classical tradition, in the collection of antique works of art and in the exact study of artefacts that forms the basis of archaeology.

The growth of archaeology as an intellectual pursuit was made possible by the revolution in thought implied in Francis Bacon's assertion that he sought understanding not from other men's words but 'by entering on the true road, submitting his mind to things'. If human reason could unlock the secrets of nature by observing phenomena and scrutinizing things, it followed that close study of artefacts should be capable of illuminating history. The breakdown of medieval Christendom and the anxiety to establish national identity supplied a powerful reason for delving into the past. It was not from idle curiosity that Henry VIII appointed John Leland as King's Antiquary in 1533. On the other hand the king fell far short of founding a national institution for the study of antiquities. The English were already too assured to feel the need to reinforce their identity. William Camden's *Britannia*, like King James's interest in Stonehenge, ministered to scholarly curiosity as much as to patriotic sentiment. Antiquarian studies were patronized by local magnates and the antiquaries themselves were mainly content with describing and delineating the ancient monuments of their localities. John Aubrey and William Stukeley concentrated on Wiltshire as Humfrey Llwyd did on Anglesey. In Britain the main driving force was scholarly curiosity rather than nationalist propaganda.

Concern with antiquities was most overtly linked with patriotic feeling in Scandinavia. In Sweden Gustavus II Adolphus chose the eve of the Thirty Years War to institute the office of Royal Antiquary which proved to mark the beginning of continuous state care of antiquities. Johan Bure (1568–1652) began the task of seeking out the ancient monuments of the country by recording the runic stones of Uppland and Vastmanland and from there went on to include a wider range of monuments over an extended territory. Bure's success encouraged the formation of an ambitious College of Antiquities based on the Gustavianum at Uppsala. The College was unique in combining the archival functions of the Royal Antiquary with the academic functions of a Professor and his assistants. Although the College itself was dissolved in 1692, the Royal Antiquary and his office moved to Stockholm where their functions have been carried on ever since.

In Denmark, as in Britain, antiquarian studies were long carried on in a spirit of scholarly curiosity. This is well seen in the case of Ole

Worm (1588–1654), whose survey of field monuments was published in the six-volume *Danicorum Monumentum*. The range of his interests is shown by the fact that his famous museum contained natural curiosities and ethnographic specimens as well as antiquities (Figure 16). It was not until the first decade of the nineteenth century that Danish archaeology was caught up in romantic nationalism. The immediate occasion was the stimulus to national pride given by the naval battle off Copenhagen and the British bombardment of the capital a few years later. Meanwhile the theft of the gold horns of Gallehus emphasized the need to safeguard national antiquities. The formation of the National Museum incorporating collections from the royal *kunstkammer* and the appointment of a Royal Commission to safeguard national monuments established a firm link between the sentiment of national identity and the relics of the Danish past. Romantic expression was given to this convergence by the distinguished archaeologist J.J.A. Worsaae in his *Primeval Antiquities of Denmark* published in 1843 and translated into English in 1849. In the English edition Worsaae averred that:

> the relics of prehistory strengthen our links with the Fatherland. We enter, through them, into a more lively empathy with hills and valleys, fields and pastures; for it is through the burial-mounds that lie humped up on their surfaces and through the prehistoric artefacts which have lain safely, down through the centuries, in their recesses, that the land can constantly remind us of the fact that our fathers, a free, independent people, have dwelt from time immemorial in this country.

Archaeology also contributed to the growth of Finno-Ugrian sentiment in the Russian Grand-Duchy of Finland. In addressing the Finnish Society of Antiquaries only four years after its foundation in 1870 the virtual founder of Finnish archaeology, J.R. Aspelin (1842–1915), advocated the formation of a National Museum in the following terms:

> The idea of a National Museum is an obvious consequence of an awakened national consciousness. The nation wants to learn to know itself and the monuments of its ancestors from bygone ages; it wants to see the fragments that remain of their struggle for their native soil, the culture and the future we have inherited. The harder the struggle, the dearer is the memory of the victors. And all these monuments which enable us to follow the struggles of our ancestors step by step through the passing centuries on the soil of our

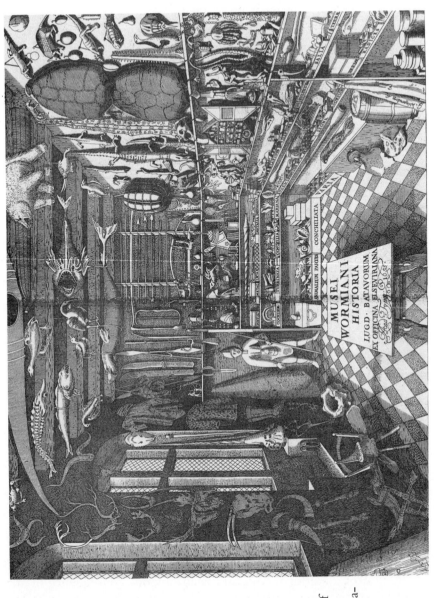

Figure 16 Ole Worm's museum, showing exhibits of varying interests – ethnographic, natural (zoological, geological) and archaeological (stone, bronze).

fatherland, belong to us, the Finnish people. We have a right to rejoice in them and the self-respect of the people and their regard for their monuments and the self-defence against outside influences, even in a political sense, too.

In recent years a similar preoccupation with archaeology as a means of nourishing national identity has marked the transition from colonial rule to independence in many parts of Africa, the Middle East and south Asia. Arrangements for protecting monuments and housing and exhibiting antiquities have been taken over from former colonial rulers and where necessary improved and improvised. Again archaeology has been introduced into the syllabus of many universities as a further means of ensuring that a knowledge of national antiquities is fully incorporated into the educational system. A similar concern for national heritage underlies requests for the return of antiquities and insistence on sharing on a basis of professional co-operation in any research projects instituted from outside. The high value attached to archaeology in many Third World countries is all the more striking in view of the pressing economic problems of certain of them. At the same time it is understandable that sacrifices should be made when in so many cases documentary sources from the pre-colonial period are inadequate to provide an historical dimension for national conscious-ness. In the Indian sub-continent the problem was more complex. Here archaeology was found invaluable as a unifying basis for societies at widely different levels of culture, some with histories longer than those of the former occupying powers, some to all intents and purposes still prehistoric. Few developments in archaeology are more impressive than the way the archaeologists of India and Pakistan have transformed our knowledge of the prehistory of the sub-continent and so created an intelligible basis for the complexities of the historical period in its several regions. The choice and retention of a design for its Service postage stamps by the government of India of one of the ornate capitals of an Asokan column is only one illustration of the pragmatic value of archaeology in promoting national unity and a sense of cultural identity.

Natural philosophical

Although national sentiment with its emphasis on cultural definition has continued to give impetus to the study of antiquity, this was heavily overlaid by the so-called European Enlightenment. Pre-occupation with local history and archaeology was increasingly supplemented by concern for mankind in the context of natural philosophy. The idea began to take shape that man and his works were the outcome of a process of continuous change. Adam Smith had already floated the idea in his *Wealth of Nations* (1763) that mankind had passed through a series of economic stages from being hunters, shepherds and agriculturalists to the stage of becoming traders and manufacturers. From a wider perspective J.C. Herder in his *Ideas Towards a Philosophy of Man* held that the universe, the earth and every form of life were the outcome of slow developments over immensely long periods of time. The human race itself was increasingly seen as the outcome of change over long ages. J.C. Prichard in his *Researches into the Physical History of Man* (1813) even invoked the process of natural selection as a likely agent of transformation. It was no coincidence that the three volumes of Charles Lyell's *Principles of Geology* (1830–3) were followed so soon by Christian Thomsen's *Ledetraad til Nordisk Oldkyndighed* (1836), the modest guide to the Copenhagen museum that opened a new phase in the history of archaeology[2] by specifying three successive ages during which Stone, Bronze and Iron were respectively the dominant materials in technology.

Although transformist ideas had already permeated several areas of knowledge for some decades, it was the publication of Charles Darwin's *The Origin of Species by Natural Selection* that signalled a decisive breakthrough for the new ideas. Its impact was greatly enhanced by the appearance of Lyell's *The Geological Evidences for the Antiquity of Man* and of T.H. Huxley's *Evidence as to Man's Place in Nature*, each of which appeared in 1863. Thomsen's three ages, which after all could easily have been accommodated within the span of Biblical chronology, offered no real challenge to accepted orthodoxies. On the other hand the notion that living forms, including man himself, had evolved over periods of geological time immensely longer than anything envisaged in human chronicles not merely opened more extended vistas to research, but presented archaeologists and anthropologists alike with well defined objectives. Above all the flood tide of evolution seemed at the time to carry the study of man into the ambit of natural science. Appreciation of the achievements of particular communities of men defined by history took second place to the elucidation of the physical, cultural and social evolution of mankind at large.

The attempt to reduce the history of mankind to a single process of evolutionary development was made along two distinct though converging routes. Archaeologists concentrated on fossil traces dating from successive periods of prehistoric time and ethnologists on the behaviour of communities still living beyond the frontiers of the modern industrial world. In combination these two lines of investigation led to the formulation during the later nineteenth and early twentieth centuries of a body of evolutionary doctrine that appeared to accord with the findings of natural science.

If the archaeologists of the Darwinian era were handicapped by having to rely on circumstantial evidence that was at the same time vestigial and derived from restricted parts of the world, at least their evidence was historically valid. Furthermore the objectives of archaeology, however difficult to attain, were hardly in doubt. Indeed a real sense of urgency had been imparted by the controversy surrounding evolution. In the very year 1859 that Darwin's book appeared we find John Evans[3] and John Prestwich visiting the Somme Valley to test the validity of Boucher de Perthe's claim to have recovered artefacts from Middle Pleistocene deposits alongside the remains of extinct animals.

The geological principle of stratigraphy was applied to the interpretation of the Late Pleistocene infill of caves as well as to settlement mounds, defensive works, burial mounds and other monuments. Systematic investigation of the French caves and rock-shelters stimulated by E. Lartet's excavations in the Dordogne[4] begun in 1863 was pursued with such expedition that by 1881 it was possible for G. de Mortillet to publish a system of classification[5] based on a complete stratigraphical sequence. The typological studies which made this possible stemmed, it should be noted, from the tradition of connoisseurship cultivated by earlier generations of antiquaries. From the outset of Lartet's careful excavations it became evident that he was uncovering a state of cultural development quite different from that revealed by settlements on the margins of Swiss lakes through a lowering of water levels during the winter of 1853/4. It was the contrast between the finds from river terraces and caves and from the lake-villages and megalithic tombs that led Sir John Lubbock to subdivide the Stone Age. In his epoch-making *Prehistoric Times, as illustrated by Ancient Remains, and the Manners and Customs of Modern Savages* (1865) Lubbock distinguished between a Palaeolithic phase during which man lived as a contemporary of extinct animals, depending on hunting, gathering and fishing and making-do with chipped flint and stone tools, and a Neolithic one marked by the adoption of farming and the practice of a technology marked by the polishing of flint, weaving and the manufacture of pottery. Although, as the full title of the book shows, Lubbock did not hesitate to fill gaps in the archaeological record by drawing on information about peoples still living at simple levels of technology, he refrained from relating them to either or both of his major divisions of the Stone Age and referred to them indifferently as savages.

Writers on ethnology were less inhibited. Carried away by evolutionary euphoria they were even ready, as Adam Smith had been, to pronounce upon what happened in the remote past without so much as putting a spade to earth or even seeking to interpret data of relevant age. E.B. Tylor even went so far as to entitle his volume of essays, published the same year as Lubbock's book, *Researches into the Early History of Mankind*. Indeed ethnologists did not hesitate to infer the stages through which human society was deemed to have passed in the course of its long history by extrapolating from information obtained in the main by amateur observers from contemporary communities still or recently living in remote parts of the world. British archaeologists were most influenced by the relatively modest scheme propounded by Tylor according to which the Palaeolithic was equated with the state of Savagery and the Neolithic with that of Barbarism, the category of Civilization being reserved for societies organized in some form of state and practising at least a degree of literacy. A wider influence was exercised on the world at large by the more ambitious formulation of the American anthropologist Lewis H. Morgan. Morgan's conviction that mankind passed through a series of definable stages of social development rested on his assumption that 'since mankind were one in origin, their career has been essentially one, running in different but uniform channels upon all continents.' Basing himself on ethnological writings, uncritical and incomplete as we can now recognize them to have been, Morgan had no compunction in asserting as a matter of certainty 'that savagery preceded barbarism in all the tribes of mankind, as barbarism is known to have preceded

Table 2 Stages in the social evolution of mankind according to Lewis H. Morgan (1877).

Societal stages	Material markers
VII Civilization	Inscriptions
VI Upper barbarism	Iron
V Middle barbarism	Domestic animals and plants
IV Lower barbarism	Pottery
III Upper savagery	Bows
II Middle savagery	Fishing, fire
I Lower savagery	

civilization'. Indeed he was prepared to be even more definite. He was even thoughtful enough in his *Ancient Society or Researches in the Lines of Human Progress from Savagery to Civilization* (1877) to provide clues for the archaeologist by citing material markers of a kind likely to survive in the soil and guide him to assign his deposits to their appropriate stage in the conjectural history of social evolution.

A correlate of the doctrine that men of the most advanced civilizations had passed through an established series of societal stages in much the same way as animal species had developed through stages of biological evolution is that peoples living outside the zone of modern industrial society could be regarded as in varying degrees primitive. That is to say they could be thought of as preserving customs and technologies discarded by more advanced societies in the course of the evolutionary process. It was this belief that made it so easy for archaeologists and ethnologists alike to compose their conjectural histories, since each felt free to borrow from the other. Archaeologists drew upon ethnological accounts of peoples fossilized so to speak at the relevant level of social evolution. By the same token ethnologists were happy to validate their stages in societal evolution by reference to archaeological sequences.

The notion that human society passed through evolutionary stages, comparable with those discerned by geologists in the history of the earth or those by which biologists derived existing species from more primitive fossils, dominated cultural anthropology for around seventy years. A main reason for this was the impetus of the idea of evolution and the weight of prestige attaching to natural science. On the other hand it lent a useful impetus to anthropology. For ethnologists it provided an hypothesis that appeared to give meaning to a mass of observations and factual data of widely varying quality that was pouring in from many sources as Europeans came into contact in a variety of ways with peoples living beyond the range of industrial society. For archaeologists it performed a similar service, extending and amplifying the Three Age System and in particular providing to some extent an instant substitute for the detailed chronological system that, although a first requirement for understanding or even plotting the course of prehistory, was not yet attainable.

The doctrine was also cherished in wider circles. It appeared to validate or at least lend countenance to two strongly held positions, namely the bourgeois idea of progress in respect of wealth and population, not to mention intellectual and moral improvement, and the Marxist gospel that human societies pass inevitably from a primitive stage through successive phases of class society, in which the state increased its power in order to protect the rights of private property, up to the timeless socialist millennium of the future. Since both philosophies, though formally opposed, were at one in being materialist to the core, it is hardly surprising that each should have found in archaeology a convenient discipline, one concerned very largely with documenting the increasing mastery of men of all cultures over their physical environments. The converse is also true. Prehistorians of the Darwinian era and far beyond have been accustomed to see in archaeology tangible evidence of material and even for a while of moral progress. It is significant that Sir John Lubbock's book of 1865, *Prehistoric Times*, included in its table of contents such entries as:

> Increase of happiness – The blessings of civilization –
> The diminution of suffering – The diminution of sin –
> The advantages of science – The future

No wonder that Sir John felt able on the penultimate page of his book, which continued to appear in new editions up till 1913, to express the sentiment that 'the most sanguine hopes for the future are justified by the whole experience of the past'.

The attitude of the founder of prehistory in its extended form was reflected in even more fulsome, not to say naive terms by Professor G.F. Scott Elliott in his book *Prehistoric Man and His Story* published by a singular irony in 1914. The author assured his readers that his book revealed

> a record of the fine achievements by which man, who was once hardly as comfortable as a squirrel or a chipmunk, rose to the peacefully luxurious condition which prevails, now and then, in most of Europe and in the United States.

In equating progress with comfort and luxury the author was a true man of his time and milieu, basking still in the afterglow of the nineteenth century. It needed the First World War to import a loftier note at least for those on the winning side. In the third edition issued in 1920 Scott Elliott accepted the defeat of Germany as sure proof that the story of man was one of moral as well as of material progress. The Preface to the new edition asserted that:

> The story of mankind is a record of continual improvement. Starting from a condition not distinguishable from that of quite an ordinary low-grade innocent sort of animal, our ancestors gradually became reasonable – moral human beings.

Finally the author felt able to conclude on his last page:

that man himself is always improving. The growth of mental ability keeps pace with the more complex environment. Not only so, but each century that passes reveals a purer morality and higher, more enlightened, ideals. We draw, then, from the story of the ascent of man, this encouraging conclusion that there is an ever-continuing improvement in humanity.

The Marxist alternative drew upon the same source. Karl Marx himself was sufficiently interested in Morgan's *Ancient Society* (1877) to take copious notes, although he did not live to use them in his own writing. It was through Friedrich Engels, notably in his *The Origin of the Family, Private Property, and the State* (1884), that this dated anthropology found its way into the Marxist canon. Although Engels derived the notion of societal stages from Morgan, he characterized them on his own terms. Supervening on a prolonged era of primitive communism he recognized the emergence of class society in three main stages. Corresponding in general with the Ancient, Medieval and Modern periods of bourgeois European historians, he distinguished slave-holding, feudal and capitalist phases, each featuring the state as a necessary means of safeguarding the property of the possessing classes. Engels rounded off his scheme by anticipating a final stage of socialism as the inevitable culmination of the entire historical process, a stage in which the state having lost its role would wither away. Each of these stages extending from the remotest period of prehistory into the future, he held to correspond to working systems, sustained by their own sets of productive forces, social relations, technologies and ideologies. The transition from one stage to another, corresponding to stratigraphical breaks in archaeological sequences, he saw as constituting the dynamic of history. A period of disruption or transition was seen as the outcome of inner contradictions disturbing the equilibrium of an existing system to the point at which it would be replaced by another better adapted to the new play of forces. Since, as Gordon Childe wrote,[6] the most numerous artefacts on which archaeologists depend were 'tools and instruments of production, characteristic of economic systems', it can readily be understood why communist states should have looked with so much favour on archaeology as a discipline. It is equally understandable that Engels' book should have 'served as a basic text-book for prehistoric archaeology in the Soviet Union'.[7] The periodization of prehistory enforced in the Institute of Moscow under the direction of N.T. Marr during the 1930s substituted social for technological labels as shown:

Table 3 Western and Marrist periodization of prehistory compared.

Conventional periodization	Societal characterization
Iron Age	Break-up of tribal society
Bronze Age	Patriarchal clan
Neolithic	Matriarchal clan
Upper Palaeolithic	Primitive community
Lower Palaeolithic	Primitive herd

Archaeological research is still planned, directed and executed in the Soviet Union and its associated states through Institutes for the History of Material Culture. On the other hand experience of the pragmatic value of patriotism during the war against Nazi Germany led Stalin to repudiate Marrism as vulgar sociology. By 1950 the wheel had come full circle. The leader of the communist world emulated the bourgeois Scandinavians of the nineteenth century in applauding the role archaeology had to play in documenting national identity. At a theoretical level the importance of recognizing archaeological evidence for the diversity of peoples was stressed and failure to do so stigmatized as a 'decolorization of the historical process'.

Cultural historical

The contemporary shift from philosophical and pseudo-historical abstraction to a more objective and systematic attempt to understand the systems by and through which human societies, whether in the present or in the remote past, have operated and still operate, though radical, has never been clear cut. Sir James Frazer continued to add new volumes to *The Golden Bough* long after A.C. Haddon and his team of specialists had demonstrated in the course of the Torres Straits expedition (1898) what could be learned from direct observation in the field of the rich cultural life of individual groups of mis-called 'primitive' people. On the archaeological side General Pitt-Rivers even managed to combine both phases in his own work: the same man who laid new foundations in Britain for systematic field archaeology with a view to unfolding the history of particular sites, assembled artefacts from all times and places and proceeded to classify them as if they were biological specimens. Perhaps the contradiction was less surprising than might appear on the surface. It was without doubt the idea of evolution, supported by a deep-seated belief in progress, that impelled archaeologists and ethnologists to undertake the rigours of fieldwork and original observation by which alone they were ultimately brought to recognize the insufficiencies of existing generalizations and the prime importance of particular patterns of culture. Anthropologists of the new era were not against generalization as such. A man like Radcliffe-Brown was concerned rather with the need to gather data sufficiently reliable to provide a basis for scientific rather than merely conjectural generalization. Conversely the prime object of fieldwork was soon seen to be the reaching beyond description to analysis and the testing of generalizations reached by means of comparative studies.

The turning point came with the resumption of active research after the end of the 1914–18 war. Taking ethnology to begin with, one can note a conscious turning away from generalizations based on evolutionary and transformist notions derived from the earth and life sciences to the direct observation of communities living at comparatively simple levels of technology beyond the contemporary frontiers of modern society. A. Radcliffe-Brown, whose monograph on *The Andaman Islanders* appeared in the same year (1922) as B. Malinowski's *Argonauts of the Pacific*, set the tone by his scornful reference to 'those anthropologists who consider it their principal task to write the history of peoples or institutions that have no history'.[8] In devoting themselves to intimate studies of remote island peoples and publishing synchronic studies of their social lives in the form of monographs these distinguished pioneers set examples that were to be widely followed. The new wave of anthropologists viewed their subjects not as 'primitive' survivors or living fossils of former stages in social evolution, but as the exponents of cultures as valid in their own way as those of their observers.

Yet, although united in essentials, not all the new anthropologists pursued the same interests. Some, impressed above all by the fragility of the marginal societies, devoted themselves first and foremost to describing, collecting and documenting cultural manifestations that were in some cases perishing before their very eyes; and who are we, in the face of such a work as A.L. Kroeber's *Handbook of the Indians of California* (1925) to doubt the value of their humility? Others, more ambitious, adopted analytical approaches. Although all such aimed to unlock the puzzle of what made the societies they studied function successfully and perpetuate themselves, they differed widely about which key they preferred to use. Some saw the most direct clues to function in social structure as this was most conveniently summarized in kinship terminology. Radcliffe-Brown admitted in so many words[9] that his encouragement of synchronic studies was not primarily designed to bring out the distinctive character of different societies so much as to provide reliable data for comparative studies. He defined his objective as being 'to arrive at valid abstractions or general ideas in terms of which the phenomena can be described and classified'. In other words, as he made crystal clear later in his lecture, Radcliffe-Brown sought

> to arrive at valid generalizations about the nature of human society, i.e. about the universal characteristics of all societies, past, present and future. It is of course, such generalizations that are meant when we speak of sociological laws.

In speaking in such terms this spokesman for British Social Anthropology was being more dogmatic than the founder of the 'structural-functional' school of Sociology himself. Talcott Parsons appreciated well enough that Sociology could only aspire to the status of a science on the basis of generalizations leading to the successful establishment of the invariant features of phenomena, but he was careful to add a rider. Having indicated that this was not difficult where phenomena are regular and repeatable, he went on to observe that this rarely applied to human affairs. The truth of this qualification has since been advertised to the world by the meagreness and banality of the generalizations which have in fact emerged at the cost of so much dedicated scholarship and financial resources. It is ironical that one of the few to emerge from Social Anthropology is that all human societies observe rules, since rules are artefacts shaped in the course of history.

Other anthropologists have emphasized the importance of economics as a way of understanding how societies operate. Sir Raymond Firth's *Primitive Economics of the New Zealand Maori* published in 1929 remains an outstanding example of this genre. Again, the very title of Audrey Richards' *Land, Labour and Diet in Northern Rhodesia* (1939) brings out the centrality of work as a key to anthropological understanding. On a neighbouring front Donald Thomson's *Economic Structure and the Ceremonial Exchange Cycle in Arnhem Land* (1949), stresses the importance of exchange as a clue to social interaction. Another extremely fruitful approach pioneered by E. Evans Pritchard in his monograph on *The Nuer* (1940) has made a point of investigating the interaction between economic and social systems and the environments in which they operate. Ecological studies of this kind provide invaluable insights into the skill with which even technologically disadvantaged communities adapt to and manipulate highly complex rhythms in the climate and animal and plant life of the ecosystems of which in a sense they form a part.

Another and quite different approach, that most clearly illustrated by Ruth Benedict's *Patterns of Culture* (1935), was founded on the *gestalt* school of psychology and based on the assumption that fully to understand cultures one needs to study their total configurations rather than focus on any particular aspect such as kinship organization or economy. Ruth Benedict appreciated that, whereas sociologists were constrained in their quest for regularities to treat all men in general terms, it was the distinctive role of anthropologists to recognize and celebrate their diversity. While it was true enough that all men in whatever society had to establish effective means of acquiring food and raw materials and develop social systems capable of maintaining group identity and ensuring their viability and perpetuation, their behaviour was in fact patterned by history.

Although the evolution of human society in the abstract may still be discussed as an academic exercise in some university departments, interest has shifted at least in the context of Cultural Anthropology to the unique character and diversity of human cultures. It is interesting to find a scholar as eminent in social studies as Clyde Kluckhohn pointing to patterned selectivity as the basis of the 'distinctiveness of each culture' and going on to identify beliefs and values as the chief factors determining the characters of particular cultures. Indeed, Kluckhohn went out of his way[10] to stress the historical dimension of culture by emphasizing the durability of value structures, even to the extent of identifying significant discontinuities in that respect with cultural change. The demolition of the view of culture as a generalized phenomenon on the model of nineteenth-century natural science has been brilliantly summed up by Clifford Geertz:

> Whatever else modern anthropology asserts . . . it is firm in the conviction that men unmodified by the customs of particular places do not in fact exist, have never existed, and most important, could not in the very nature of the case exist.[11]

The development of archaeology as a constructive historical discipline was quite as much inhibited by the euphoria of evolutionary doctrine as was that of ethnology as a means of gaining an insight into the way different human societies in fact operated. The main impediment was the illusion that categories proper to natural science could appropriately be applied to the study of man as a cultural being. The fallacy that fossils of human behaviour were amenable to interpretation as if they were geological or palaeontological specimens was a direct legacy of the revolution in thought accomplished or at least brought to a head by Darwin, Huxley and Lyell. This can be seen clearly enough in Sir John Lubbock's *Prehistoric Times* in which the author claimed specifically that, just as the fossils of extinct animals can only be understood by comparing them with representatives still living in other continents, so

> in the same manner, if we wish clearly to understand the antiquities of Europe, we must compare them with the rude implements and weapons still, or until lately, used by the savage races in other parts of the world. In fact, the Van Diemaner and South American are to the antiquary what the opossum and the sloth are to the geologist. [12]

Since as we have seen the whole possibility of an expanded vision of antiquity of the kind unfolded by Lubbock was due in large measure to the euphoria generated by Huxley and his circle, sentiments such as these were only to be expected in 1865. Again, it is hardly to be wondered at that the ideas which generated such a fruitful period in the history of archaeological research should have persisted long enough to impede the onset of a new phase in the development of prehistory. This was all the more so that they were invested with the prestige of natural science and warmed by the glow of the idea of progress or the approach of the Marxist millennium. Even a pioneer of systematic field archaeology like General Pitt-Rivers was still stating forty years on that 'the existing races, in their respective stages of progression may be taken as the bona fide representatives of the races of antiquity.' [13]

On the other hand it is significant that the last influential author to maintain such a position was a professional geologist. As late as 1926 the Professor of Geology at Oxford continued to seek ethnographic parallels for the peoples responsible for fabricating the artefacts from successive stages of the Palaeolithic sequence and, conversely, looking for the archaeological counterparts of primitive peoples living or until recently living in more or less remote parts of the world. Sollas even went to the length of maintaining that the recent Tasmanians represent

> with great probability . . . an ancient Mousterian race which cut off from free communication with the surrounding world had pre-served almost unchanged the habits and industrial arts which existed during the later days of the Lower Monastirian age. [14]

If archaeology was to contribute in a worthwhile manner to an appreciation of the way men developed during the immensely long and profoundly significant ages of preliteracy, it could do so only as a historical discipline, emphatically not as a branch of natural science. Whereas geology and palaeontology were in essence abstract and generalizing in so far as they were contributing in a substantial way to natural science, the prehistory of human societies had of necessity to be concrete and to particularize since it was dealing with the products of specific historical traditions. As Gordon Childe once perceptively expressed it, 'Prehistory cannot be content with an abstract humanity.' It was ineluctably concerned with a plenitude of societies each constituted by the transmission of unique cultural patterns. When prehistoric archaeology entered on its great period of expansion between the wars of 1914–18 and 1939–45 it was influenced in part by the example of the leading field anthropologists of the time, but in large measure also by scholars trained in the humanities who accepted as a matter of course that they were faced with a diversity of distinct peoples. This certainly applied to Gordon Childe himself. As he made explicit in the opening paragraph of his epoch-making *The Dawn of European Civilization* (1925) he came to the subject with the prime aim of understanding the genesis of 'European civilization as a peculiar and individual manifestation of the human spirit'. One of the first things he discovered as he examined the archaeological data in detail was the range of cultural diversity present in different parts of the continent at any particular period. This he brought out in a series of profoundly influential maps, each defining the territorial extent of cultural groupings as these were indicated by recurring associations of archaeological traits, including pottery, burial rites and particular forms of implement, weapon or ornament. The persistent recurrence of such assemblages defined for Childe the extent of the communities constituted by history which he termed cultures.

Childe was fully aware that the old stadial mentality was built into the very concepts, language and classifications of prehistorians. He saw the need to point the moral of his practical essays in culture-based archaeology by precept as well as by example. Even ten years after *The Dawn* it was still necessary to labour the need to break away from the abstract approach of natural science to the interpretation of historical data. The nineteenth century fallacy that impeded archaeology was to seek to apply categories adequate for natural phenomena to products of the historical process. As Childe emphasized: 'Prehistory cannot be content with an abstract humanity. It cannot reach the individual, but it can appreciate the differences between nation and nation, differences due to distinct social traditions.'[15] Childe was able to invoke incontestable evidence for diversities of cultural expression at different periods of the Later Stone and Bronze Ages of the European continent. He was even able to note the beginnings of radical change in the assessment of the Old Stone Age, the very core of the old stadial classification. Here the lead had already been taken by Dorothy Garrod whose own fieldwork went some way to showing that de Mortillet's system was only valid for parts of western Europe. Every extension of the geographical range of Palaeolithic research made the parochial nature of the French sequence more apparent. Even before the 1939–45 war Miss Garrod's work in Palestine and Mesopotamia and that of Czech, German and Rumanian prehistorians in central and eastern Europe, not to mention that of Soviet excavators over immense tracts of the USSR, had demonstrated that diverse patterns of cultural expression had already grown up at least as far back as the Upper Pleistocene, even within a limited part of the Old World.[16] The world-wide expansion of prehistoric research since the war, together with the greater definition made possible by modern scientific and technical aids, has brought cultural diversity into ever greater prominence as a key index of human achievement.

In reviewing, however briefly, the reaction against stadial notions based on false analogies with the natural sciences, it has been emphasized that archaeologists and ethnologists alike encountered a rich diversity of cultural expression when they engaged in close observation and research in the field. This does not mean that they abandoned all hope of making valid generalizations. On the contrary Radcliffe-Brown, as we have seen, merely wanted to ensure that he used valid data rather than conjecture as a basis for generalization. In the case of prehistoric archaeology Gordon Childe's example is of particular interest, since he brought to the subject two distinct and in some ways conflicting prepossessions, a Marxist concern for generalization and a scholarly interest in the unique character of European civilization. Although it amused him from time to time to test the social-stadial terminology devised by Tylor and Morgan against the raw data of archaeology,[17] he showed himself aware all along that the material he dealt with as a prehistorian was the product of 'specific societies, each with its own distinctive history'.[18] At the very end of his life he made his position even clearer when in the penultimate paragraph of his 'Valediction' he wrote:

> The Marrists' appeal to 'uniformities of social evolution' while it seemed to make intelligible the development of each individual culture to which they applied it, completely failed to explain the differences between one culture and another and indeed obliterated or dismissed as irrelevant the differences observed.[19]

If one asks how far recognition of the uniqueness and diversity of human cultures has undermined the idea of progress, the answer must depend on perspective. Restricted to the narrow band of time mirrored in the records of literate civilizations based on polities that by their nature were precarious and fragile, the answer can be read plainly enough in the mute traces revealed by archaeologists as they dig through their successive ruins. It is only if one takes account of the unwritten but several thousand times longer record of prehistory that it is possible to return a more hopeful answer. As Charles Singer implied we now have a new and more reliable yardstick for defining progress. With every advance in prehistoric research it becomes more practicable to chart distances on the road of humanization in terms of the very fossils of human achievement. To this extent it is becoming possible, as it is for some purposes even useful, to speak and think of the overall progress of mankind.[20]

To begin with, the archaeological record documents in overwhelming abundance a cumulative advance in technology, in the capacity to exploit natural resources and in building up the body of practical knowledge from which abstract science ultimately developed. The fact that technology has steadily accumulated despite the fall as well as the rise of civilizations, so that useful innovations have been incorporated into the conventional wisdom even when the cultures responsible for them have long since vanished, is an outcome of diffusion.[21] The phenomenon of diffusion, at least on the scale on which it operates in human society, points to one of the most profound differences in the potentialities of men and other animals. Whereas biological adaptations perish when species become extinct, innovations in culture can readily be transmitted by means of language, writing or electronic media, not to mention by actual exchange of artefacts, to any community ready to receive them. It should be emphasized at this point that worthwhile diffusion between groups can only occur where distinct cultural traditions still exist. Cultural diversity is an essential prerequisite for the operation of one of the most vital processes in the maintenance and development of civilization, much as the genetic diversity embodied in primitive cultivars and wild plants is a vital resource for cross-fertilizing existing cultivated species. Without differences there can hardly be interaction and without interaction lies death.

During the first flush of enthusiasm, it was widely assumed that an irrefutable biological indicator exists for measuring human progress in the growth and concentration of population. Already we find Sir John Lubbock accepting as axiomatic that 'if any animal increases in numbers it must be because the conditions are becoming more favourable to it' and from there going on to remark that 'population as a rule increases with civilization'.[22] Even Childe, who so frequently pointed to the fallacy of applying biological criteria to cultural phenomena, could write that 'multiplication of the species' was the 'final test of progress' and one all the more useful because susceptible of measurement.[23] Today our position is rather different. It is not merely that in writing prehistory unilinear stages of economic development have been widely eschewed and even such landmarks as the 'Neolithic Revolution' flattened.[24] The very notion that biological success could be accepted as a sufficient index of progress without reference to the quality of human life is under challenge where it has not been abandoned. One of the most taxing problems facing governments today is not how to increase or concentrate, but how to limit and disperse populations. Even at a biological level further increases in the density of population are viewed as threats to health and nutrition, hardly as signs of progress. It is now part of the conventional wisdom that human progress can only be measured in human, that is in cultural terms.

One area in which overall progress can certainly be inferred lies in the enlargement and deepening of conscious awareness. In some fields, notably the graphic arts and burial rituals, this can be demonstrated or at least illustrated by a wealth of archaeological data. Awareness of the past can first be documented when inscriptions begin to appear in the archaeological record. On the other hand, as we know from the customs of preliterate peoples the world over, there are many ways of storing knowledge of the past, few of which could leave direct traces in the soil. Mime, dancing, poetry, drama, not to mention the recital of genealogies and legends, are only some such media for conserving and heightening a common sense of the past. One reason for the ubiquity of this sense is its adaptive value in promoting survival. A sense of the past increased the effectiveness of those who shared it by enhancing self-confidence. By helping to validate customs and social structures it intensified social cohesion by stressing what members of the community had inherited in common. Again, it reinforced a sense of identity *vis-à-vis* groups with different histories. A final point to make is that like all other aspects of life and thought it was subject to selective pressures. The range and depth of historical awareness is conditioned to a significant degree by what is relevant to social needs. Where small numbers of people supported relatively simple technologies the spatial boundaries of their historical awareness would be limited to the territories they exploited themselves, supplemented by more impressionistic references to areas within reach of more distant exchange networks. Similarly their temporal range would be restricted for most purposes to the experience of parents and grandparents supplemented by references to more remote or even mythical ancestors incorporated in oral tradition. It was only as social structures grew more complex that men experienced the need for a more extended view of the past. On the other hand the fact that they felt a need to know about more extended territories or longer spans of time by no means lessened their interest in more local or domestic frames of reference. In other words hierarchy developed increasingly in respect of historical awareness as it did in society itself. The mere fact that geographical and astronomical exploration gradually brought the whole world and in a remoter way the universe within the cognizance of men has in no way reduced the value to them of accurate knowledge of their more immediate environments. By the same token, the formation of national or imperial states did not eliminate the need for regional, parochial or even familial frames of reference. No more has the unfolding of world prehistory during recent generations destroyed or even impaired concern for the many dimensions of recorded history by which communities sustain their cohesion and identity. What archaeology has done is to enlarge the perspective from which men are able to visualize their situation. It reminds us that we have attained our present degree of self-awareness by shaping and elaborating the astonishingly diverse cultures whose material embodiments provide the archaeologist with his documentation and all men with direct insights into what it means to be human.

4
The genesis of cultural diversity

Human culture taken as a whole may be described as the process of man's progressive self-liberation.

ERNST CASSIRER[1]

It has been argued that we owe our humanity to membership of communities enriched and patterned through the transmission and reception of cultural traditions. Further, that despite suggestive correspondences we differ from our closest living relatives in the animal world to the extent that our basic instincts and genetic endowments are overlaid by our cultural heritage. Our identity as human beings is held to depend above all on our self-conscious awareness of what it means to live in a moral as well as a physical world. Whereas at one level, the level we share with other animals, our lives are almost entirely conditioned by our genetic inheritance, at the human level, the level at which in Benjamin Disraeli's words 'man is conscious that he is made in God's own image',[2] the predominant influence is that exerted by the cultural inheritance acquired from society. The only continuous record of the cultural way of life in past ages is that provided by archaeology. Although the evidence is highly incomplete, not to say vestigial, and reflects some aspects of life in much greater detail than others, archaeology provides an impressive body of historical information. It is our only source for the immensely long prehistoric period. For the historical period it can often amplify and occasionally check the evidence available in documents. With all its drawbacks archaeological evidence has the supreme merit of being tangible. It is capable of being directly measured and quantified. Yet it is also capable of conveying in a very direct manner nuances of style and standards of excellence. It is able to throw light on any aspect of behaviour that leaves material traces. Above all it allows comparative judgements to be made, not merely about the material efficiency of cultures, but also and more significantly for certain purposes about the rules and values which in the last resort mark the true distinction between the human way of life and that of the brutes.

There are two highly significant ways in which the cultural heritage of human societies differs from the genetic inheritance of animal species. There is a marked difference in the degree of dynamism, innovation and change. It is true that organisms are subject to mutations which affect their genetic endowment. Without this after all the evolution of species could hardly have occurred. On the other hand as the fossil record shows – *Australopithecus robustus* has already been cited in this regard – once animal species were fully developed they were liable to breed true to type over periods measured in geological time, until overtaken by drastic ecological change or more effective competitors. By contrast the dynamic potential of cultural endowment is witnessed by the entire course of human history. Whatever the fate of particular communities or social units, the course of history is continuous. Yet its essence and in the final analysis the only thing that makes it worth studying is the fact of change, the tempo of change and the forms taken by change. The second way in which the dynamism of culture is manifested in history rests in the propensity to diversify. Here again the contrast between human and animal society is both profound and revealing. Whereas animal species of their very nature breed true to type, it is of the essence of human culture that it is not only capable of rapid change under certain conditions, but also of an unlimited number of local variations and diversifications. Since the connection between change and diversity in the field of culture is so close – they are in effect only two aspects of the same phenomenon – their underlying causes will be discussed together.

As a matter of convenience the ecological and economic factors which may have triggered and channelled change and diversification will be reviewed before passing to what are conceived to be more fundamental causes stemming from the nature of the cultural way of life. As a preliminary it may be worth recalling that the social structures and cultural patterns by which human communities functioned were as much subject to the selective process as were the biological endowments of organisms in the course of the evolutionary process. The process of competition selected in favour of those arrangements that were more as against those that were less effective. It is true enough, and one illustration of the difference between men and other animals, that human societies could always choose to satisfy non-material values at the cost of economic efficiency. There would be little point in cherishing cultural values if this were not so. On the other hand it has to be remembered that values which run counter to economic trends have to be paid for at some cost and that in practice these could only be afforded in narrow limits by communities whose economic margins were as narrowly drawn as they were for most of human history. Societies which impaired their effectiveness beyond a certain point might find it difficult to compete with ones not so handicapped in terms of survival. Again, the point could soon be reached beyond which members would cease to be willing to pay the cost. Cultural patterns and social systems, one may conclude, can only be maintained in so far as they can compete effectively with rivals and at the same time retain the acceptance of their constituents. If either of these imperatives could not be met survival could only be ensured at the price of adaptation and change. And, although history shows that this was often belied in the event, the best hypothesis is that the desire to survive is sufficiently overriding to prevail in most cases over the reluctance to change.

One of the basic requirements for stability lay in harmonious relationships between social systems and the habitats and biomes in which they operated (Figure 17).[3] Relations established within an ecosystem comprising a human community, terrain, climate and animal and plant life are liable to be upset by disturbances in any one dimension. The concept of an ecological equilibrium has its uses but only as an analytical tool: in real life ecosystems are dynamic, veritable theatres of change. Changes in any dimension of the natural environment are likely to call for cultural adaptation and, given the interdependence of the several components of social systems, this is likely to involve matters far removed from those immediately affected. Thus climatic fluctuations are likely to call for some response from technology, settlement and broad areas of social life as well as from patterns of subsistence. Again, economic change may have a more or less pronounced impact on the environment and back again: extensive forest clearance that commonly resulted from the practice of agriculture

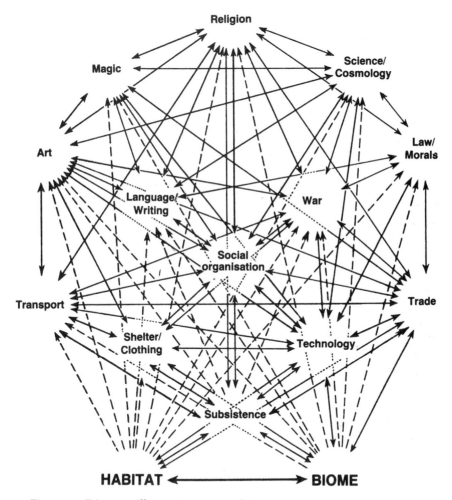

Figure 17 Diagram illustrating some of the reciprocal relations obtaining between different areas of social life and the main components of the environment, the whole forming a working ecosystem.

is only one way in which economic life might transform the environment in ways which called for further adjustments in the cultural sphere. It needs to be remembered furthermore that farming no more existed in the abstract than any other social activity. Research makes it ever plainer that the adoption of agriculture and stock-raising only marked a climax of working relationships established by particular groups of people in particular habitats over periods of time extending in some cases over tens of thousands of generations. It is already plain that, although animals and plants and farming practices were certainly spread over new territories by a process of diffusion, the process of domestication and the development of farming regimes was passed through in many different parts of the world and involved many different species requiring distinct methods of cultivation and herd management. Indeed it is a sound hypothesis that the adoption of farming in different parts of the world must in itself have been a major factor making for cultural diversity in the course of Neothermal times.

At a deeper level two factors may be invoked in seeking to account for growing diversification in the field of culture. The first of these, already touched upon when discussing some of the more significant differences between men and their closest living relatives, resides in the greater degree of freedom experienced by men as they emerged from the thraldom of instinctive behavioural patterns programmed by their genes. In Friedrich Hegel's estimation men experienced a kind of spiritual emancipation as they passed from a purely biological state of being to one consciously shaped by history, a point of view well summarized in a sentence of Ernst Cassirer's quoted at the head of this chapter. Self-liberation and emancipation are of the utmost relevance to our immediate theme, since they underscore the possibility of choice. The ability to define alternatives and make the most beneficial choices went hand in hand with the enhanced ability to reason that distinguished men from the other animals. Yet it would be to give an entirely wrong impression of ancient society to imagine that change was of the order of the day. The forces of conservatism that make it possible for societies to cohere, endure and transmit their values to future generations were strongest precisely where the cultural endowment was at its most elementary: men clung the more tenaciously to what little they had. Social acceptance is at all times an essential prerequisite for effective cultural change. It is fair to assume that under the conditions obtaining during the Stone Age this would only have been forthcoming when the existing system had demonstrably broken down or at least revealed noticeable deficiencies of a kind that could only be remedied by change. The significant fact remains that when such a situation did arise new ideas, under normal circumstances suppressed, were always available in human societies. Thanks above all to articulate speech, another feature unique to human society, their merits could always be expounded to overcome reluctance. Not all human groups responded appropriately or promptly enough to avoid disaster. On the other hand the archaeological data embodying prehistory testifies to man's ability to respond effectively to change. The fact of diffusion was another feature that helped to distinguish human from animal societies. Artefacts, raw materials and by a fair inference ideas were capable of moving rapidly and over long distances even during the Stone Age. Communities were bombarded by ideas emanating from far beyond the body of their own members.

Another weighty factor making for diversification of culture stemmed from the self-conscious sense of identity that characterized human societies. The integrity of animal species was a part of their biological endowment. Individuals bred exclusively within the species and if for no other reason could recognize each other by a variety of physical and behavioural characteristics. Among men on the other hand a sense of identity was highly self-conscious. It was recognized in the final analysis as the most important fact of existence. It was projected back into the past and symbolized in every artefact made to serve the needs of the present. Furthermore its prolongation into the future was regarded as one of the principal objects of social institutions and beliefs. The converse of awareness of identity was a hardly less insistent sense of separateness from other societies having their own distinct identities. To interpret the institutions, concepts and artefacts incorporated in the archaeological record as components of working systems is necessary and correct, but totally insufficient for full understanding. The symbolic meaning of culture is at least as crucial. If for example one takes a given assemblage of pottery it is generally possible to classify it in terms of widespread functional categories such as vessels for cooking, storage, eating or serving food or pouring liquids. When it comes to assigning it to a particular group on the other hand the archaeologist relies on characteristics of style, finish and ornamentation which symbolize and express adherence to cultural entities. As in the case of social behaviour or belief systems, so in the fabrication and ornamentation of artefacts, whether made from flint, stone, metal, fired clay or organic materials and intended for domestic purposes, hunting, fighting or ceremonial use, the adherents of different cultures selected from alternatives and created patterns they could recognize as distinctive of their own group. The self-conscious diversification of culture that stemmed from this way of enhancing a sense of corporate identity was from an evolutionary point of view adaptive in three distinct though complementary senses. It enhanced the cohesion and self-assurance without which communities could hardly remain human, while at the same time alerting them to alien and potentially hostile groups and enriching the fruits of interaction between distinct traditions through contact and diffusion.

Before reviewing the operation of the various factors making for cultural change and diversity among prehistoric communities in terms of the archaeological evidence, it is important to stress that the process was subject to the general law that change tends to accelerate in time. This is nowhere more conclusively exemplified than in the perspectives offered by prehistory. Whereas during the earliest stages the tempo of change was so unimaginably slow that it could be measured in geological terms, by the close of prehistoric times archaeological periods, equivalent to intervals of relative cultural stability, were as a rule too short to be usefully measured by radiocarbon dating.

Table 4 Comparative duration of major phases of prehistory in western Europe.

Approximate duration in years	*Major archaeological periods*
500/600	Pre-Roman Iron Age
1,000	Bronze Age
2,000	Neolithic
4,000	Mesolithic
22,000	Upper Palaeolithic
40,000/50,000	Middle Palaeolithic
500,000/2,000,000	Lower Palaeolithic

Note The figures are very approximate.

Even this crude profile of the rate of change measured in technology is enough to illustrate the rate of upturn experienced in the course of prehistoric times. Change was barely perceptible in the well stratified sequences of east Africa dating from the Lower and Middle Pleistocene. The first notable acceleration began in association with the appearance of *Homo sapiens* during the latter half of the Upper Pleistocene. Such a profile is entirely consistent with the hypothesis that human industrial activity reflected a process which one might expect to have been as long drawn out, yet as self-sustaining and cumulative, as that of humanization. By the same token it is hardly surprising that assemblages of artefacts embodying the earliest essays in culture of which tangible records survive should have been so nearly uniform as the instinctive behavioural patterns they reinforced and progressively replaced. The stone tools of the Lower Pleistocene were of so elementary a character, comprising as they did little more than flakes and nodules, that they offered only minimal scope for detectable variation. This hardly applied to the much more sophisticated implements that appeared during the Middle Pleistocene, namely hand-axes shaped by flaking nodules or thick flakes on either face in such a way as to provide them with regular working edges extending round much of the perimeter. Technically these hand-axes were in some cases among the finest artefacts ever made in flint or stone. Yet they were so uniform in style over territories extending from southern Europe to the Cape and the Indian sub-continent (Figure 18) that our leading authority on the Lower Palaeolithic, Professor Desmond Clark, was led to comment that:

One of the most striking things . . . about the broad pattern of the

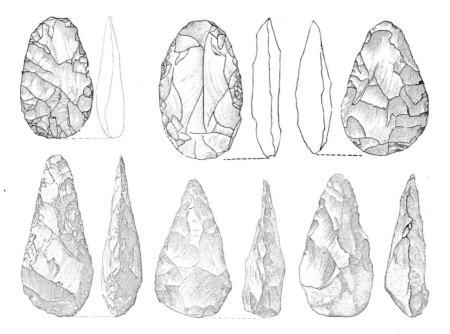

Figure 18 Hand-axes of ovate and pointed forms from (*left to right*) Europe, Africa and India.

Middle Pleistocene is its general 'sameness' within the limits imposed by the stone industries. . . . Hand-axes from Europe, South Africa, or peninsular India are all basically similar tools, and this is also true for the rest of the heavy-duty and the light-duty elements.[4]

Even allowing for the fact that Acheulian hand-axe industries were confined to the same relatively warm zone as their forbears and within this primarily to grasslands and savannah, the degree of uniformity in what were now quite sophisticated products is impressive. Like the slow tempo of change the relatively marked degree of homogeneity of early artefact assemblages reflects the expected gradualness of the process of humanization itself. One indeed fed the other. The slow rate of change and high degree of uniformity were functionally related: the slower cultural development was in its early stages, the more effectively such innovations as did arise locally were able to diffuse over the territory as a whole and so reinforce the appearance of uniformity.

If we are right to approve the view that *Homo sapiens* emerged to some degree as a product of cultural adaptation, it is no surprise to find that the first decisive acceleration in the tempo of cultural change dates from the same era as early fossils of the new species of man. It is also interesting that both developments proceeded at a time of expansion into previously unoccupied ecological niches. Such an expansion was in itself liable to stimulate change as different elements of the socio-cultural heritage sought to establish working relationships with novel habitats and biomes. The process of adaptation and change unfolded in part in the course of effecting a more complete occupation of territories previously settled on a selective basis and in part as an outcome of expansion into new territories beyond those previously colonized by man. The first of these can be most conveniently documented for Africa. South of the Sahara the makers of hand-axes of Acheulian type continued to exploit the resources of grasslands and savannah to which they were accustomed and in which they had grown up. It was when they began to colonize previously neglected forest zones[5] that the outcome of adapting to novel ecological conditions became apparent in the archaeological record, notably in the lithic industries of Sangoan type characterized by heavy bifaces, picks and push-planes. The Sangoan inventory is commonly accepted as indicative of tree-felling and timber-working. Indeed it could well be that the lithic material that bulks so prominently in the archaeological record was mainly preparatory and that most of the tool-kit and gear used by the Sangoans was in fact made of wood.

The spread of man over all the main continental areas from the warmer territories of Africa and southern Europe and Asia, where he had first emerged as a genus and undergone the long-drawn-out earlier phases in his cultural evolution, was accomplished while he was still gaining his living from hunting, fishing and foraging. The colonization of vast new areas with widely varying environments during the latter half of the Upper Pleistocene exemplified the dynamic possibilities inherent in culture (Figure 19). Whereas other animals, while by no means lacking in ability to adapt, were genetically programmed to cope with limited ecological ranges, men were able by means of their culture to adapt to almost any environment. The only limitation imposed on them in any particular context was their technology and it was precisely this that was most readily capable of adjustment and change. What is at all events certain is that modern man dramatically expanded his habitat during the latter part of the Upper Pleistocene. The line of expansion to Australia from east Asia by way of Indonesia,[6] still largely conjectural in its early stages, but increasingly well documented in its continent of arrival, is most likely to have been accomplished at the time when sea-levels were substantially lower and gaps between the islands correspondingly shorter.

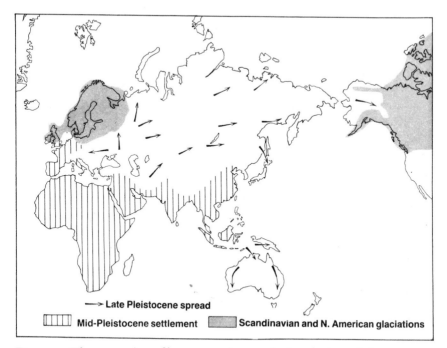

→ Late Pleistocene spread

Mid-Pleistocene settlement   Scandinavian and N. American glaciations

Figure 19 The expansion of human settlement during the Late Pleistocene.

Although if this were so the expansion need not imply any sophisticated form of navigation, it nevertheless suggests that early man was prepared to improvise even at a simple level of technology. A second and in some respects even more dramatic expansion involved the colonization of northern and east Eurasia, Japan and the New World. The northward movement in the USSR round the southern and eastern margins of the Scandinavian ice-sheet was initiated by Neanderthal man and maintained by his Upper Palaeolithic successors.[7] Archaeological evidence secured by Soviet prehistorians provides unambiguous evidence of some of the cultural advances that made this possible. Traces of tent-like structures made of skins stretched over poles supported by boulders or heavy animal bones have been uncovered at several localities in the Ukraine associated with artefacts of Upper Palaeolithic age. One of the best preserved foundations is that discovered at Mezhirich, composed of an oval setting of mammoth bones enclosing some 23 square metres (Figure 20).[8] There is also suggestive evidence for warm clothing, including a realistic figurine of a person clad in a fur garment and hood from Buret, Siberia. As well as spreading down the valleys of rivers flowing into the Arctic, the Late-glacial hunters penetrated Japan[9] and further north occupied the

Figure 20 The foundations of an Upper Palaeolithic dwelling at Mezhirich, Ukraine, formed largely of mammoth jaws.

plain of Beringia which then joined the extreme east of the USSR with the ice-free parts of north America, including much of Alaska and the Yukon.[10] The breaking of the glacial barrier to expansion further south which occurred when the Cordilleran and Laurentide ice-sheets parted opened up immense territories teeming with game. Pressing forward the Paleoindian hunters fanned out reaching the Atlantic seaboard and pushed south, through Mexico and on into South America where with astonishing speed they reached as far as the Magellan Strait.[11] Before ever a grain of wheat had been sown or a domestic cow milked man had inherited the whole world apart from islands dotting the oceans, adapting to an immense range of environments through the medium of his culture. This he was able to accomplish in part by more skilful manipulation of his existing stock of technology, but in part also no doubt by innovations that brought with them a greater range of diversity.

Quite apart from their geographical expansion the men of this time displayed evidence of inventiveness in many fields which led in sum to an enhanced degree of cultural diversity. Innovations in equipment reflecting rapid changes and marked local differentiation have been keenly observed by archaeologists for the sound reason that they served to define temporal phases and regional cultures. Particularly clear examples are afforded by hunting gear which, because it served the vital purpose of securing prey, was among the components of technology of most significance for prehistoric man as well as for those who study his archaeological traces. Change and diversity in weapon armatures were so pronounced in Upper Palaeolithic times even in a territory as restricted as western Europe that prehistorians have seized upon them as keys to cave sequences. Thus, the split-base bone point was taken as a key fossil for the Middle and the tanged flint of Font Robert type for the Late Aurignacian phase. The delicate flint points flaked on both faces that more than anything else marked the succeeding Solutrean cultural phase displayed marked regional differences in their later stages. This is particularly true of Spain where Cantabria and Asturias favoured shouldered points, Catalonia stemmed points and Valencia delicate barbed and tanged arrowheads among other forms. The final or Magdalenian stage of the western cave sequence showed a marked interest in forms of projectile head made from antler (Figure 21). These included composite forms with forked heads fitted to bevelled foreshafts, curved points with lateral flattening which probably served as barbed tips and a varied sequence of harpoon-heads barbed on one or both edges. A radically different type of weapon head provided with sharp cutting edges formed by

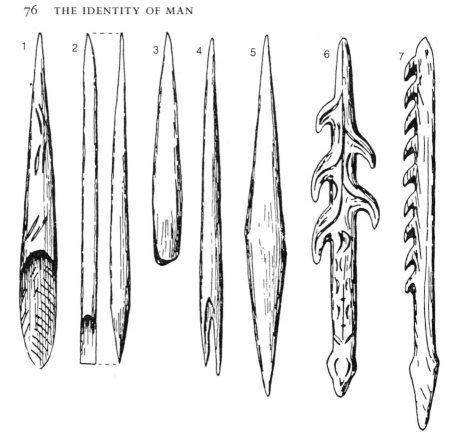

Figure 21 Diverse projectile heads of antler and bone, Upper Palaeolithic Europe. 1, 2 single and double bevelled points. 3 split-base point. 4 forked base point. 5 lozenge-shaped point. 6, 7 barbed antler harpoon heads, biserial and uniserial.

inserting flint bladelets into lateral grooves was almost certainly developed in Eurasia, though ultimately extending from Scandinavia to the circumpolar zone of the New World. An outstanding illustration of the way a basic form could undergo innovation and diversification is provided by the stone projectile points originally introduced to North America as bifacially flaked leaf-shaped forms of the kind distributed from the Yukon to Mexico, Venezuela and even the Argentine. The most notable innovation made by the Paloeindians was to remove flakes from the base along the median axis in such a way as to provide a groove or fluting, the function of which was presumably to keep the head more securely fitted to its shaft.[12] In the case of Clovis points the fluting was restricted to the lower part of the point, but in the mitre-shaped points of Folsom type it might extend almost

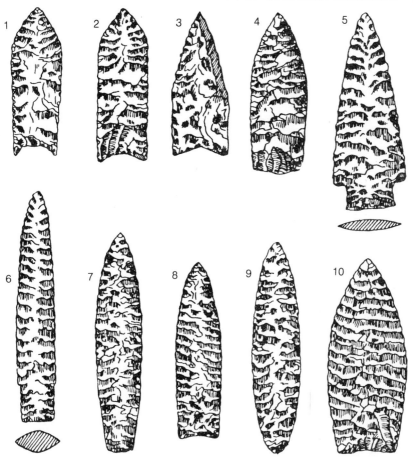

Figure 22 Diversity of bifacially flaked stone projectile points developed
by the Plains Indians of North America during Neothermal times. The
forms illustrated comprise those termed 1 Midland. 2 Plainview.
3 Meserve. 4 Milnesand. 5 Scottsbluff. 6 Eden. 7 Angostura. 8,
9 Agate Basin. 10 Browns valley.

to the tip. In environments like the Plains region big game continued
to form the basis of the food quest well into Neothermal times and the
spear and spear-thrower continued to play a key role. Plano points
were still flaked delicately over either face, although no longer fluted,
and their beauty of form so captured the imagination of modern
collectors that they have defined and named numerous varieties
(Figure 22). Although not all these distinctions are widely accepted
there can be no question that a large number of standard shapes were
perfected by the prehistoric Indians of the Plains region. It would be

absurd to seek to explain the manifold varieties of Plano point as adaptations to local ecology, since the basic leaf form was widespread, nor again is it feasible to interpret them in functional terms. Rather should we interpret them as symbolizing social identities, defining groups conforming to specific cultural traditions and flourishing in particular territories over specific periods of time.

If the exploitation of previously untouched ecological niches, the colonization of vast new territories including those where colder climates prevailed and the systematic hunting of an increasingly wide range of animals with more effective gear all helped to promote cultural change, the domestication of animals and plants worked in the same direction. The radical change in subsistence which this ultimately brought about exerted its main influence by greatly facilitating the widespread adoption of a sedentary mode of life. Before turning to this it may be noted that paradoxically it also made possible the virtual completion of man's expansion over the world, notably through the colonization of the small island groups of Polynesia scattered widely over the Pacific ocean. This it did in two ways. It contributed the technology needed for the canoes that carried the voyagers, their families and food stocks over such vast distances. The polished stone adzes, which dominate Polynesian archaeology and were used to fabricate not only canoes but a variety of houses, images, weapons, handles, combs and containers, were originally developed along with axes for clearing forest and making the more permanent and often larger dwellings associated with farming. The war canoes of the Maori solidly constructed by lashing timber strakes either side of a dugout hull were splendid products of disciplined labour and thanks to skilled dovetailing of sections at prow and stern might exceed twenty-four metres in length. A second requirement, not merely for the voyages but for sustenance in the new homelands, was the assured supplies of food that only domestic animals and plants were able to guarantee. Each of the domestic animals carried overseas in the canoes – dog, pig and jungle cock – were of Asian origin and the same applies to all the cultivars other than the sweet potato which may have spread from the New World at a comparatively late stage. Species brought from Asia included banana, breadfruit, coconut, gourds, taro and yams. Not all of these were carried to or at least cultivated in all the island groups colonized by man. Yet the last three reached New Zealand even if their cultivation was only practicable on the North Island.

Geographical expansion into new environments and the domestication of animals and plants both involved profound changes in ecological and economic circumstances. Yet it would be a mistake to imagine that such changes of themselves determined cultural reactions. Their role was rather to offer new scope for the many factors making for change and diversity inherent in the culturally dominated way of life by which modern man was shaped and in which he still lives and has his being. A point already made about the economic transformation implied by farming but which can hardly be stressed too often or too strongly, is how far it was from being a mere phase in the abstract social development of mankind proclaimed by nineteenth-century evolutionists. On the contrary it was something experienced many times and in different parts of the world, on each occasion under unique circumstances. The 'Neolithic Revolution' attributed to the Middle East and which was held to have transformed economic life over much of Europe and north Africa, was in fact only a local dramatization by western prehistorians of a world-wide process.[13] Wherever and whenever human societies based their economies on the domestication of particular groups of animals and plants, the outcome was to some degree unique, since it involved regimes of cultivation, stock-raising and settlement adapted to the soils, climate and topography of a particular habitat and the properties of the various species concerned. This can only have made for the emergence of economic regimes adapted to the unique circumstances prevailing in different centres, regimes which must surely have influenced patterns of settlement and technology and in this way provided settings for enhanced diversity of culture.

Yet it would be wrong to lay too much stress on the direct impact on culture of varying patterns of subsistence. The true significance of the transition from hunter-foraging to farming economies for the diversification of culture stemmed rather from its general implications. Any improvement in food-raising that ensured the security of food supplies, permitted a greater density and aggregation of population and encouraged a more sedentary mode of life created conditions under which the underlying forces making for diversity were given greater scope to influence cultural development. The need for a secure home base was, as we saw earlier, experienced from an early stage of humanization and increasingly so as the process accelerated. On the other hand among hunter-foragers the need to take the fullest advantage of animal breeding cycles and the seasonal ripening of plant products compelled seasonal movement unless under exceptional conditions. A crucial advantage of regimes based on domestication was that food resources could be concentrated the year round within the immediate proximity of permanent settlements. The greater fixity of settlement generally available through the practice of farming had a multiplier effect. Crops grown adjacent to settlements profited from the rich nutriment represented by food residues and other organic waste stemming both from human populations and their dependent herds. The greater security in food supply that came from eliminating the uncertainties inherent in catching activities and on the other hand the positive advantages enjoyed by farmers, through being able both to accumulate a wealth of meat in the form of living herds under immediate control and to store plant food and notably certain cereals and root crops at actual settlements, made it possible and safe for substantially larger numbers of people to live regularly together: instead of hunting-bands of fifteen to twenty-five people, it became possible for the first time for men to settle in village communities with ten or twenty times that number.

Larger communities further increased the possibilities for a subdivision of labour beyond and cutting across those stemming from merely biological categories of age and sex. This in itself together with the bare fact of being stationary meant the rise of new crafts whose products were in some cases peculiarly susceptible to diversification. Some of these, textiles being one, were too perishable to survive commonly enough for more than occasional comparative studies. Pottery on the other hand was perfectly adapted to receive and record the imprint of cultural identity. While still in a plastic state it was amenable to fabrication in a variety of shapes and susceptible to decoration by several different methods and in a variety of styles (Figure 23). Once fired on the other hand it was extremely resistant to decay. This and the fact that its manufacture was so widespread among settled populations as to be almost an index of sedentarism meant that pottery has served as possibly the most reliable indicator of cultural change and diversity. Among other crafts to develop in the context of settled communities, notably in many parts of Asia and Europe, copper and bronze metallurgy played a prominent role as offering a conspicuous medium for expressing identity and displaying diversity.

The greater range of crafts practised in settled communities certainly provided new outlets, but the decisive factor making for increased diversity of culture was surely the enhanced consciousness that came from living permanently in larger communities rooted in and exploiting narrowly defined territories. Another factor in promoting a sense of identity that grew in importance as the wealth made possible by a sedentary way of life accumulated was the increasing need to defend property. Although Neolithic settlements are commonly defined, they were not as a rule provided with elaborate or

Figure 23 Diversity in Neolithic Greek pottery, a succession of ceramic styles in Thessaly. 1 Dhimini style. 2 Sesklo style. 3 Early block and linear style.

substantial defences. These and a parallel development of specialized armament first became evident as wealth, embodied for example in copper, bronze and gold, accumulated. This was a continuing and on the whole an accelerating process. The heightening of the sense of identity and of distinctiveness from other groups nourished by competition and the threat of conflict was intensified by the mere fact that it became increasingly necessary for survival. Cultural diversity under such conditions was increasingly of adaptive value.

If the differences in cultural expression between Stone Age peasant communities were less strikingly evident than that say between the architecture of the Ming and Moghul empires, they were nevertheless perceptible enough to prehistorians to form a much used basis of classification. When Gordon Childe sought to describe the early peasant societies of Europe in *The Dawn of European Civilization* he took as his basic units the constituents of the mosaic of cultures which he claimed to descry at successive periods between (in his chronology) the Vth and the IInd millennia BC. In writing of cultures Childe referred to reflections in the archaeological record of coherent and often repeated patterns of behaviour shared by historically constituted communities. The territories occupied by such cultures he defined by plotting the distribution of diagnostic traits, relating to such aspects as subsistence, settlement and house forms, technology, ornaments, art, styles, religion and disposal of the dead. Since 1925 when Childe first published his seminal book the question how archaeological cultures should be defined, even whether the concept itself is any longer useful, has been a matter of earnest methodological debate. The fact remains that Childe's maps reflect a real phenomenon, namely that the early European peasantries, still largely Neolithic although increasingly practising copper metallurgy, displayed a variety of styles so well defined that first year undergraduates could be taught to assign archaeological assemblages to their correct culture grouping and thus to their correct geographical and chronological provenance.

What Childe observed for the later stages of European prehistory, others have found elsewhere as archaeology expanded its geographical range. It is now evident that rapid change accompanied by the diversification of cultural traditions has been going forward all over the world since the later phases of the Upper Pleistocene. The process of humanization did not advance in the generalized or uniform manner of a geological process. Instead it assumed many guises. These took on even sharper definition in the hierarchically structured societies that began to leave written records and so to inaugurate the historical era. The nature of the change from prehistoric to early historic societies may be easier to appreciate in terms of the transitional forms defined by Elman Service[14] as chiefdoms. These could no longer be described as tribal and yet had not attained the degree of organization we generally expect to find in the literate polities that in the Old World qualify as civilizations. Yet they show a notable advance in the specialization of labour and hence in the organization of redistribution. They were commonly marked by the formation of centres at which economic, social and often religious activities were co-ordinated and by the emergence of leaders able to operate the system by prestige and to defend it by military prowess.

Chieftains in the sense used by Service presided over the petty realms with shifting boundaries which existed immediately before and after the Roman occupation during the Celtic (La Tène)[15] and Anglo-Saxon phases[16] in the cultural history of southern England. Archaeological material such as treasures buried during the pre-Roman period and no less strikingly the royal ship burial of Sutton Hoo reveals a pronounced difference in wealth between chieftains and the common people. By contrast with those found on settlements or average cemeteries, artefacts from the rich finds were made of materials so costly and to standards of workmanship so refined as to cause astonishment to those who in our own age gaze upon them in museums or are privileged to subject them to closer scrutiny. Such

Figure 24 Teutonic interlaced ornament on the great gold buckle from an Anglo-Saxon ship burial at Sutton Hoo, England.

things can only have been made in workshops with traditions of specialized craftsmen working for patrons intent on defining their superior status. The amount of gold incorporated in chieftains' finery is impressive. The six La Tène torcs from the Ipswich hoard weighed approaching or slightly over a kilogramme each, ranging from 858 to 1044 g, even if only some four-fifths was pure gold (Figure 24). The great buckle from Sutton Hoo, although weighing less than half as much (412 g) as each of the Ipswich torcs and having only a marginally higher gold content, formed only a quarter of the total weight of gold objects in the burial.

The objects from La Tène treasures and the Sutton Hoo burial focus on personal finery, warlike equipment and appurtenances of feasting. The forms chosen for display and still more the styles in which they were shaped and decorated on the other hand exhibit to an enhanced degree the cultural diversity which existed between the Celtic and Teutonic worlds. Chieftains of both cultures used brooches and bracelets, though of different forms, but torcs or neck ornaments seem to have been special to the Celts and buckles to the Anglo-Saxons (Figure 25). Again, mirrors which the Celts derived from Roman prototypes in Gaul and used as vehicles for La Tène art do not seem to have appealed to the Anglo-Saxons. In respect of weaponry both laid stress on swords, helmets and shields, but only the Celts went in for

Figure 25 Bronze mirror decorated in curvilinear Celtic style from Desborough, England.

decorative horse-trappings and chariot fittings. Feasting and enter-
tainment were a common resource for maintaining high state and both
Celts and Anglo-Saxons emphasized cauldrons and their suspension
gear as well as drinking horns. As usually happened diversity in
decorative art found its greatest scope in prestigious objects made to
enhance the status of leading patrons. In aiming to do this Celtic
craftsmen drew upon their prehistoric inheritance for geometric
designs, took floral elements from archaic Greek sources and animals
and animal and human masks from the east, and transmuted this
amalgam into a magical style of their own invention. Teutonic
craftsmen depended more heavily on the east. From there they derived
the animal style, which Swedish craftsmen elaborated to form interlaced ornament, and the love for strong colour which they satisfied by
inlaying coloured glass and garnets. The contrast between the two
styles can be made more effectively visually than in words by comparing the Desborough mirror with the great gold buckle from Sutton
Hoo.

5
The findings of ethnography

In the beginning God gave to every people a cup of clay, and from this cup they drank their life.

PROVERB OF THE DIGGER INDIANS OF CALIFORNIA

Another and quite independent way of gaining an insight into the lives of non-literate societies based on traditional cultures is to see how peoples beyond the frontiers of the modern industrial world were conducting themselves when they first came under the observation of western man. The obvious source for this is the evidence of ethnography. Archaeology, as we have seen, is capable of providing a tangible record of the process of humanization from the first steps taken by the earliest Primates recognizable as men. It has already given us an outline fossil record of the emergence and diversification of the cultural traditions by which men achieved their identity as men. Yet, like all evidence comprised by fossils that of archaeology is incomplete, partial and often enigmatic. The modes of thought, the languages, the social arrangements and the values of the societies fossilized in the archaeological record are no longer there to help us to interpret what we recover from the soil. The ethnographic evidence, although in itself incomplete and subject to misinterpretation, complements that of archaeology to the extent that it is based on the study of communities still functioning as living entities down to the day before yesterday.

Before seeing what this new source of information can tell us, something should be said about its nature. Ethnographic evidence varies in quality as well as in kind. A clear distinction needs to be drawn between that derived from the observation of indigenous peoples at the time of initial contact with western man and that recorded after their ways of life had to a greater or less degree been modified or even transformed through acculturation. Although strictly speaking the notion of purely indigenous or native cultures is something of a fiction, since ideas have shown themselves throughout history to have been capable of penetrating cultural boundaries by one kind of diffusion or another, there can hardly be any doubt that it was contacts as close as those involved in trading, fighting, missionary activity and colonial administration that brought about the radical transformations which in our own time have gone far to obliterate indigenous patterns of culture over large parts of the world. Indeed it is evident that by the time they were closely studied by professional anthropologists, many cultures were already to some degree influenced by western contacts. It is now reasonably clear that many features of what had only recently passed as traditional Maori culture were in fact creations of the colonial period. For instance the introduction of iron tools profoundly modified the technique and styles of wood carving, previously carried out by stone tools; again, the introduction of fire-arms, apart from its direct impact on the layout of defensive works, by intensifying rivalries among chiefs had a significant effect on other dimensions of Maori culture.

A second and in some respects more significant factor to be borne in mind when interpreting ethnographic evidence is the competence of those responsible for collecting or recording it. During the initial phase of contact the records on which we depend were for obvious reasons obtained in most cases by observers lacking expertise in ethnology and not infrequently of limited general education. Their written accounts were for the most part anecdotal and failed to address themselves to many of the questions about which we would most like to be informed. On the other hand in so far as they were factual and descriptive such written accounts as we have from the period of initial discovery can be accepted as primary evidence which can often be made to yield fuller information when viewed in the light of later analytical studies by professional anthropologists. Certainly they were in many cases of much more value than the writings of venerated 'fathers' of anthropology compiled at second or third hand to buttress preconceived notions of stadial evolution. By the time anthropologists trained to analyse the operations and structures of human communities had taken the field the non-industrial societies they had come to study had already been more or less radically transformed. Yet the more analytical and critical approach of modern social anthropologists has contributed immeasurably to our understanding and not least of the process of acculturation. Indeed, it is only through the insights of professional anthropologists that we can appreciate how it is that communities with apparently simple technologies have been able to maintain effective and satisfying ways of life down to recent times even under physical circumstances that could daunt western man despite his ostensibly 'more advanced' culture.

A third point to remember about ethnographic evidence is that in addition to written accounts, it includes the drawings and latterly the photographs by which observers documented their notes. Furthermore it includes artefacts collected more or less systematically both as confirmation of field notes and as independent sources of evidence. It has to be admitted that the iconographic evidence has to some degree been adulterated by illustrations made to flatter the prejudices of people living at home in the comforts of western civilization. On the other hand many illustrations were made at or close to the time of discovery as part of the basic records of explorers and voyagers. Before the days of photography the standard of draughtsmanship was generally excellent and pictorial records made at the time of first contact must surely rank highly as sources when adequately documented. In the present context a few examples of the contributions made by draughtsmen to the ethnographic record must suffice. Some of the most dramatic pictorial records were made in the course of Captain Cook's voyages. The importance attached to pictorial records is shown by the fact that in joining the *Endeavour* for Cook's first voyage (1768–71) the redoubtable Joseph Banks took aboard two professional draughtsmen (Sydney Parkinson and Alexander Buchan) as well as his private secretary (Herman Spöring) who was also a skilled delineator,[1] not to mention four trained collectors.

The illustrations brought back by explorers and voyagers – and the French were extremely active at this time – were not incidental but carefully planned as part of a comprehensive record. Although Banks' draughtsmen were much occupied in recording natural history specimens they each contributed significant records of Maori life, including in Spöring's case meticulous renderings of the carvings on their canoes (Figure 26), all the more precious as they preceded colonial settlement. For sheer integrity in the rendering of detail it would be difficult to beat the illustrations made by John Webber who sailed on Captain Cook's third voyage (1776–80). In particular Webber is notable for his delineations of people in the context of houses and settlements. His views of the interior of a Maori fortified settlement or *pa* dating for 1777 and of a village scene in Hawaii dating for the following year are precious documents[2] of life in the Pacific during the pre-colonial period. Equally invaluable are the meticulous records he made on Nootka Sound, Vancouver, discovered by Cook during his quest for the northwest passage. Through the medium of Webber's drawings one receives an impression of life in the interiors of the great houses of the northwest coast Indians[3] in the year of their discovery (1778) far more vivid and in some respects more detailed than one would be

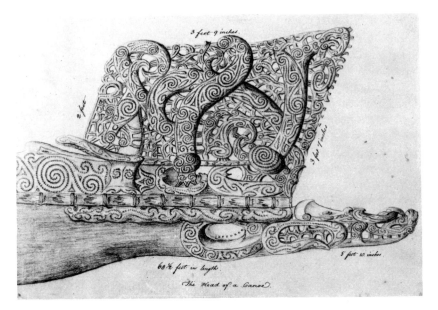

Figure 26 Prow ornament of Maori wooden canoe recorded by Joseph Banks' secretary on the first of Captain Cook's voyages in 1770.

likely to receive from written accounts alone (Figure 27). The voyage of the *Beagle* (1832–6) provides another familiar example.[4] In addition to the official artist (Conrad Martens) both Captain Fitzroy himself and Midshipman Philip King were accomplished draughtsmen. Between them they added usefully to the ethnographic pictorial records of Tahiti, New Zealand, New South Wales, Tasmania and Tierra del Fuego. It would be wrong to give the impression that voyagers overseas were the only explorers to add to the pictorial records of the immediate ethnographic past. In Australia, to take only one example, those who, after an initial period of consolidation following on Governor Phillip's settlement at Sydney (1788), progressively opened up the interior of the continent, made notable contributions to the pictorial record of aboriginal life while still relatively uncontaminated by western contacts. The illustrations of aboriginal burial monuments and practices published in John Oxley's account of what he saw as he penetrated the interior of New South Wales during the second decade of the nineteenth century still speak to us today.[5] The tradition set by the pioneers of Australian ethnography has not been lost upon their modern successors. In few countries has the camera been put to better use than in Australia for recording the ecological adaptations and ecology of aboriginal groups still or until very recently exploiting habitats in which few white men could survive without imported rations: the superb photographs by Donald Thomson[6] and latterly by Richard Gould speak for themselves,[7] though it is fair to stress how much they gain from the theoretical insights of the distinguished anthropologists who took them.

The most tangible evidence for the cultural attainments of traditional societies beyond the range of the modern industrial world is comprised by the artefacts they were actually using at the time of their discovery by western man. Unhappily only a small proportion of the material originally collected and brought back to Europe can certainly be identified in existing ethnographic museums. There are several reasons for this. Scanty attention has until recently been paid to the proper cataloguing and study of ethnographic material. In Britain more than anywhere professional anthropologists have chosen to concentrate on social topics. The insights contributed by social anthropology are admittedly vital for an intelligent appreciation of ethnographic data. The fact remains that an almost exclusive concentration on the social dimension has deprived museum studies of the finance and trained scholarship needed to overcome the often deplorable state of some of the key ethnographic collections. This arose in part from the low priority attached by most museum men during the

Figure 27 The interior of an Indian house at Nootka Sound, Vancouver, as sketched by John Webber in 1778.

nineteenth century to 'primitive' artefacts as opposed to those documenting national antiquities or the high civilizations of antiquity. Another reason was the haphazard manner in which collections were too often dispersed on the return of expeditions and voyages. The rich materials brought home by Captain Cook are a case in point. As a recent assessment of the fate of the artefacts brought back from his first and second voyages indicates, no systematic attempt seems to have been made to distribute them in the interest of scholarship. When the ships returned, the ethnographic collections, which unlike the natural history specimens were not systematically catalogued, were distributed widely among friends and patrons. Indeed enterprising individuals seem to have furnished their cabinets by purchasing direct from crew members as the ships docked. Nevertheless substantial numbers of objects ultimately found their way to the British Museum in addition to Joseph Banks' own benefaction. Yet what has been described as the most important single collection of Hawaiian material was acquired by Göttingen and other items came to rest in Berne and Vienna, not to mention New Orleans and Wellington, New Zealand. It is all the sadder that so relatively few of the British Museum specimens can be attributed with certainty to one or the other of the Cook expeditions.[8] In this respect the Museum is better placed in respect of the rich material collected from Nootka Sound at the time of its discovery.[9] In some cases, for example the Maori material collected on the same expedition and now at Cambridge, the story is even happier. It seems evident that Joseph Banks was fond of distributing specimens to his aristocratic friends, in this case the Earl of Sandwich and Thomas Pennant. The bulk of the collection of thirty-six pieces now in the University Museum of Archaeology and Ethnology at Cambridge was transferred to it at its foundation from Trinity College, to whom Lord Sandwich had passed the collection presented to him by Banks as early as 1771, the remainder coming ultimately from the Tennant collection. In view of its character and pedigree this collection of Maori artefacts dating from the period of first contact has been rightly described as 'a document of the highest importance',[10] a judgement which applies whether one chooses to think of it as documenting the ethnographic past or, what in effect amounts to the same thing, the final phase of Maori prehistory.

By and large communities with the most elementary economies survived longest in territories most remote from and ecologically unattractive to peoples with more powerful ones. The fullest anthropological studies of peoples practising economies based on hunting, fishing and foraging have been made in territories like the Kalahari or the deserts of west central Australia too arid for farming, in tropical forest zones like Amazonia, the Congo or Malaya, or, again, in the frozen territories of the Arctic zone. There, in habitats too extreme to attract more than marginal and belated attention from western man, anthropologists have made the most of opportunities which have by now mostly disappeared. One of the first lessons to stand out from their studies is the capacity shown by members of a variety of racial types, all of them it is important to remember belonging to the same species as we do, to exploit almost the whole range of the most extreme environments to be found on earth. They owed this to the almost infinite adaptability of their cultural apparatus. A vivid impression of the range of cultural adaptation encountered by ethnographers may be had by comparing hunter-foragers of aboriginal Australia with the Eskimo hunter-fishers strung out across the circumpolar zone between Alaska, Greenland and Labrador. By contrast with aborigines having little or no clothing, the flimsiest of shelters and no more equipment than could conveniently be carried on foot together with infants over the more or less extensive territories exploited during the annual cycle, the Eskimos devised skin clothing of remarkable sophistication, wooden goggles with narrow eye-slits to reduce snow-glare, a variety of house forms, ingenious and highly efficacious equipment for hunting and catching birds, fish and mammals under a variety of land, sea and ice conditions and not least dog-sledges for traversing ice and snow and skin boats for sea transport and marine hunting.[11] Over a territory as extensive as that of the Eskimos it is hardly surprising that, despite overall similarities, variations existed in the material equipment encountered by ethnographers. The way these ingenious people adapted to the extremities of Arctic conditions has been studied most fully in the central area extending from the northern zone of the Hudson Bay region to Baffin Land. In his study of the Iglulik Eskimos, Therkel Mathiassen[12] provides telling descriptions of their material culture including the means they took to protect themselves against temperatures which for long periods average less than $-40°C$ and occasionally fall below $-50°C$. An obvious requisite is clothing warm enough to withstand such temperatures but which at the same time permits the freedom of movement demanded by hunting, fishing and travel. The Eskimo invest heavily in materials and skills. A man's winter clothing for instance requires eight complete caribou skins to make inner and outer frocks with hoods, inner and outer trousers and stockings, and in addition boots and mittens, each and all made by sewing together ingeniously and accurately cut components (Figure 28). No less attention is paid to the design and construction of dwellings. Here, as in clothing, seasonal variations of climate involve distinct adaptations to meet changing conditions. The winter version is again chosen for comment as illustrating Eskimo capability in the face of the most severe conditions. The dome-shaped snow house or igloo built of blocks of snow has rightly been described as a marvel of Eskimo technique. Caught in a snow storm at temperatures of $-40°$ or $-50°$C the Iglulik Eskimos are able in the course of an hour to 'create a house in which one may live warmly and comfortably while storm and frost rage outside'. As Mathiassen went on to point out it was mainly because they had not learned to build snow houses that pioneers of European stock were so immobile in winter. But the snow house was much more than a contrivance for emergencies. Provided with a sealskin lining and often comprising several interconnected chambers with windows made from slabs of ice they might serve to shelter up to four families throughout the winter (Figure 29). The body warmth of the inhabitants together with the heat generated by burning blubber lamps raised temperatures up to $5°$ and $6°$C above zero. This in turn melted the inner face of the snow domes which on freezing became so strong that men could stamp on them without damage.

Human societies differ from animal species not merely in being able to adapt by means of culture to the widest range of environments found on earth: they are also capable of adapting in quite different ways to the same or similar environments. Neither habitat nor biome nor the ecosystem as a whole determine the cultural patterns that shape human behaviour. They merely set limits and these ecological limits were in turn constrained by the cultural capital available to each society. What might be precluded for those with weak economies might on the other hand be possible for those with stronger ones. In other words the way human societies adapt to their environments is largely conditioned by history, by their cultural antecedents and by the extent to which they have profited from diffusion from other social traditions some of them more advanced in particular fields. Not surprisingly anthropologists have been able to observe what prehistorians have only been able to infer, namely that cultural diversity exists even at the basic ecological level. As Daryll Forde laid down in his well-known text book, 'in regions closely similar in relief, climate, and vegetation sharply contrasted types of human life are to be found.'[13]

Detailed anthropological studies have shown that aboriginal populations, however elementary their material equipment, habitually classify their environment and its resources by means of vocabularies

Figure 28 Iglulik
Eskimo man's outer
dress made from soft
caribou skins sewn
together.

relevant to their particular modes of life. The Wik Monkan people of Cape York Peninsula, Queensland were found by Donald Thomson[14] to recognize five seasonal phases and to name a large number of plants and forms of animal life on which they depended for subsistence and raw materials. Whereas farmers exist by the intensive exploitation of relatively few species, hunter-foragers as a rule draw upon a much larger variety. To take the most effective advantage of wild food resources such people needed to acquire and transmit a detailed knowledge of the breeding cycles and periods of maximum vulnerability of a more or less extensive range of mammals, birds and fish as well as the most profitable time to gather and collect an even wider range of plants, insects and molluscs, not to mention the most effective ways of catching, harvesting, storing, preparing and cooking these varied foodstuffs. The full potential of such numerous and varied resources could only be realized by means of a more or less intricate scheduling of the food quest over annual territories that were commonly too extensive to be exploited from a single base and thus involved seasonal movements. The rhythm was commonly set by fluctuations of climate, notably in territories where seasons of heavy rainfall alternated with drought or prolonged winters, with ice-

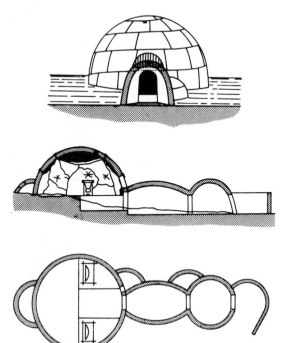

Figure 29 Eskimo snow house, Davis Strait, northern Canada.

covered seas being broken by brief summer thaws. Studies by ecologically orientated anthropologists like those made by Donald Thomson on the Wik Monkan, by Evans-Pritchard on the cattle-keeping Nuer of the Sudan[15] or latterly by William Fitzhugh on the Eskimo groups of Hamilton Inlet, Labrador (Figure 30),[16] have revealed cycles that extend far beyond mere food-procurement or the activities connected with this, including means of travel and transport, weapons, gear and utensils. Furthermore the necessity for seasonal movement and variations in climate and the availability of abundant supplies of food meant that the numbers aggregated in single settlements varied as well as the nature of houses or shelters. This in turn affected the programming of ritual activities associated with such social occasions as initiation ceremonies and marriages. Similarly seasons of dearth tended under certain circumstances to influence the timing of raiding activities. A point that needs to be stressed is that subsistence-settlement systems could be seen when studied in detail to be to a certain extent unique to particular social groups even within a territory as relatively small as Hamilton Inlet about 150 miles long and some 30 miles wide.

Peoples with seemingly elementary equipment have shown themselves not only able to survive but positively to flourish in environments into which ethnographers only penetrated for short periods and then with the backing of vastly more impressive resources. As Richard Lee has shown from his painstaking study of the 'Kung Bushmen[17] these hunter-foragers apparently only need to work two and a half days a week to sustain what seem to them satisfying lives in what appears to us as the hostile environment of the Kalahari desert. The Bushmen, like the hunter-foragers so sympathetically observed by Richard Gould in the deserts of west central Australia, have succeeded in part it is true through the support they receive from their mythology and social institutions and rituals but in large measure also through detailed knowledge of their habitat and of the animals and plants on which they depend for their living. A measure of the success of so-called primitive peoples as applied by ecologists is the relative failure of western man to compete on level terms. A trivial illustration, but one reported intermittently in the Australian press, is the fate of motorists, often city-dwellers and not unseldom recent immigrants, whose cars break down in the desert. Too often they die of thirst where an aborigine would experience no great difficulty in finding water. On a more epic scale is the famous story of the Norse settlement established on the west Greenland coast in 986.[18] Although the settlers managed to establish some 280 farms, 16 churches and a

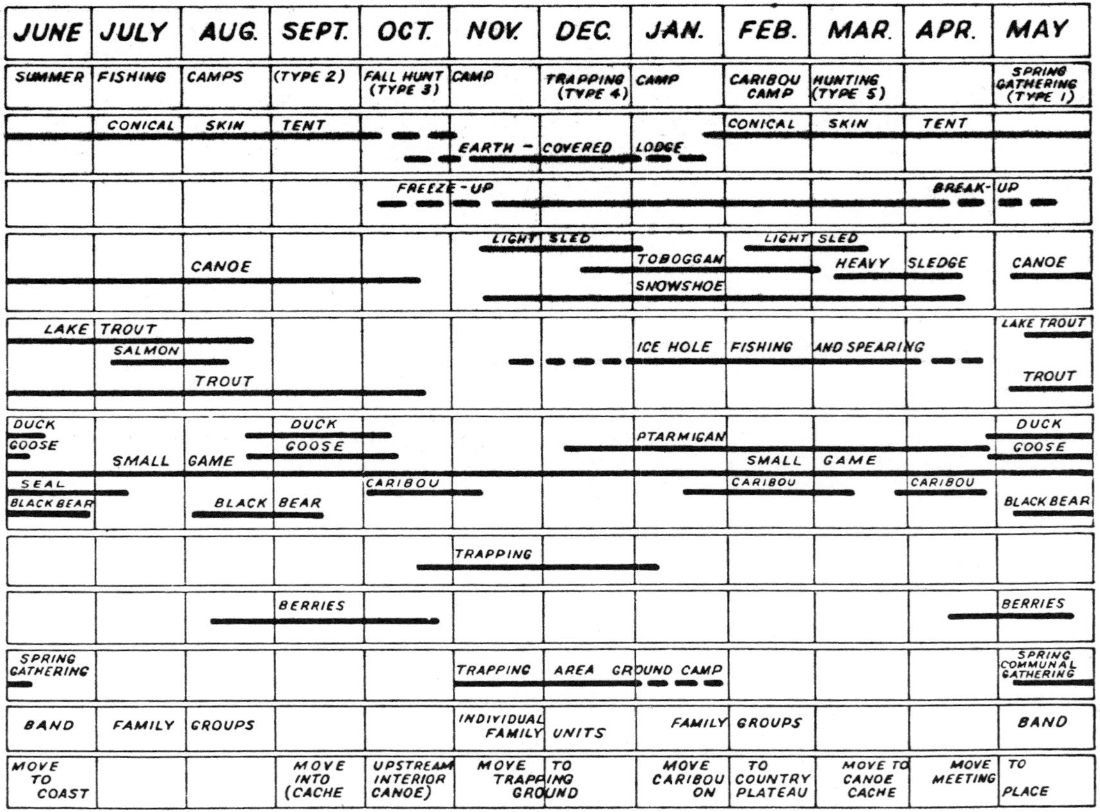

	JUNE	JULY	AUG.	SEPT.	OCT.	NOV.	DEC.	JAN.	FEB.	MAR.	APR.	MAY
Camp type	SUMMER	FISHING	CAMPS	(TYPE 2)	FALL HUNT (TYPE 3)	CAMP	TRAPPING (TYPE 4)	CAMP	CARIBOU CAMP	HUNTING (TYPE 5)		SPRING GATHERING (TYPE 1)
Dwelling		CONICAL	SKIN	TENT	EARTH – COVERED LODGE			CONICAL	SKIN	TENT		
Ice					FREEZE-UP						BREAK-UP	
Transport			CANOE		LIGHT SLED			TOBOGGAN / SNOWSHOE	LIGHT SLED	HEAVY SLEDGE		CANOE
Fishing	LAKE TROUT / SALMON		TROUT				ICE HOLE FISHING AND SPEARING					LAKE TROUT / TROUT
Birds / small game	DUCK GOOSE	SMALL GAME		DUCK GOOSE				PTARMIGAN	SMALL GAME			DUCK GOOSE
Large game	SEAL / BLACK BEAR		BLACK BEAR		CARIBOU				CARIBOU			BLACK BEAR
Trapping						TRAPPING						
Berries				BERRIES								BERRIES
Gathering	SPRING GATHERING					TRAPPING AREA GROUND CAMP						SPRING COMMUNAL GATHERING
Social unit	BAND	FAMILY GROUPS			INDIVIDUAL FAMILY UNITS				FAMILY GROUPS			BAND
Movement	MOVE TO COAST			MOVE INTO (CACHE)	UPSTREAM INTERIOR (CANOE)	MOVE TO TRAPPING GROUND		MOVE CARIBOU ON	TO COUNTRY PLATEAU	MOVE TO CANOE CACHE	MOVE TO MEETING PLACE	

Figure 30 Annual cycle of economic activities practised by the North West River band of the Montagnais–Naskapi Indians of Labrador.

Norwegian episcopal see, they never succeeded in 500 years in making themselves independent of their links with Scandinavia. Consequently, when communications broke down with the home base their fate was sealed. Already during the latter part of the fourteenth century the Eskimos began to attack their settlements from the north By around 1500 the Norse settlers had finally succumbed to the indigenous population. The Eskimos, heathen though they were, unable to read and lacking European technology, were nevertheless infinitely better adapted not merely to survive but to flourish on their own resources under Arctic conditions into which even now Europeans only venture with support from their own homelands. It is all the sadder to reflect that the satisfaction derived from their success in adapting to extreme environments has not saved them from the impact of more developed societies in recent times. Among the Australian aborigines studied by Gould it was the desire to possess iron axes that more than anything undermined their integrity and rapidly brought about the destruction of their culture. If iron axes and degradation seem a poor exchange for the Garden of Eden, the Australian aborigines are far from being the only people to have made the same mistake.

The material equipment needed to secure and prepare food, to move easily over the habitat, provide clothing and shelter and to ensure adequate defence, to mention only some of the more basic needs of human society, all provide media for expressing diversity. Some degree of diversity can be accounted for in terms of adaptation to differing ecological or economic circumstances. On the other hand much of the diversity in material culture encountered by ethnographers requires different explanations. In part these arise from cultural history. Inventions whose value might be thought to transcend ecological circumstances have been found as a matter of fact to be unevenly distributed. Here one has to take account of culture history: the diffusion of certain traits may be for some reason restricted or even have failed to gain acceptance by particular cultures. The bow does not appear to have been in use among the Australian aborigines at the time of contact with Europeans. Again, many of the basic requirements of human societies could equally well be met by any of a variety of means. Containers made of bark, basketry, animal skin or wood could be quite as effective as pottery and under nomadic conditions very much more convenient. But this is only part of the story. Even a cursory inspection of well displayed ethnographic collections will show that equipment made by different groups for the same purpose differs widely not merely in the materials used, in themselves largely a function of ecology and economy, but also in form and style, in other words in cultural expression. Where the material collected from particular groups is exhibited together it is not uncommon to find a common style extending to the total range. Conversely in the Pitt-Rivers Museum at Oxford, where the arrangement of the collections in accord with the General's ideas has been preserved and the various categories of artefact, whether it be containers or weapons, are abstracted from their cultural settings and exhibited together, the significance of cultural preference is made even more immediately apparent. This applies not merely to technique and form, but frequently also to the decorative motifs engraved, carved, inlaid, or in the form of bead-work, feathers or other materials. Although in describing these it is usual to treat them as though they were purely decorative, when ethnographers have studied a particular human group in depth they are sometimes able to show that in fact they carry meanings of a social, ritual or religious order to the people who made and used them. Research has indeed shown that what is formally the same motif may carry quite different meanings to different groups and contrariwise that the same basic idea may be conveyed by quite distinct motifs among different social groups. Whatever the product, in tribal societies artefacts serve, apart from their utilitarian function, the overriding purpose of strengthening and defining the identity of the social groups by means of which culture is transmitted and men achieve and experience their humanity.

In some respects the most telling symbols of men's anxiety to identify with social communities and at the same time define their status within them are to be found in the lengths they have gone to modify their own bodies and personal appearance. Although western man still engages to a limited degree in similar practices, we find it difficult not to characterize as other than bizarre some of the more prized manifestations of other societies. If western ethnographers describe as deformations and mutilations what to their practitioners are viewed as personal enhancements and badges of social identity, this only helps to illustrate the astonishing range of diversity in taste. Even a bare enumeration of practices would require fuller treatment than can be given here. As examples one need only mention such customs as modifying the shape of the skull in infancy by applying bandages or head-boards or inhibiting the growth of foot-bones by tight binding; removing fingers at certain joints; knocking out teeth or alternatively filing or blackening them; boring the nose for inserting plugs, rings or skewers; distending the lips to receive plugs, that might be of portentous size and highly dysfunctional character; and piercing the ear-lobes, sometimes as a preliminary to distending them to reach the shoulder. Among modifications that many people may find it easier to accept as embellishments one may include tatooing by means of punctuation (Figure 31), scarification by scar-forming cuts, the painting of face, body and nails and the dyeing and more or less elaborate dressing of the hair.

Personal ornaments in the form of extraneous objects attached to the body by suspension, fastened to the limbs or attached by perforation of the ears, nose or lips were another closely associated medium for signalling group identity and individual status. Indeed the possibilities in respect of artificial ornaments were even greater than in respect of modifications to the body itself. As one writer has neatly summarized the position, an immensely wide range of raw materials was drawn upon to make

> ornaments attached to heads, necks, arms, legs and waists, and worn as headbands or tiaras, necklaces, armlets, bracelets, bangles and finger-rings, as belts and girdles, leglets, anklets and toe-rings in indescribable variety.[19]

Clothing was yet another medium to signal a wide range of diversity between human communities and classes. Although clothing designed for Arctic conditions, like Eskimo skin garments, were doubtless devised to keep men and women sufficiently warm to operate out of doors in extremely low temperatures, an environmental explanation will hardly apply to regions too warm for clothing to be necessary. In the warm climates where man originated and many of the tribal groups most closely studied by ethnographers exist some other explanation must apply. A likely hypothesis is that garments were in origin mere elaborations or amplifications of bodily ornaments. What ethnographers have in any case been confronted with is a variety in styles of clothing almost as bewildering as those displayed by personal ornaments. A vivid illustration may be quoted from European folk culture as this existed into the later nineteenth century, still survives in some localities for festive occasions or, sadly, is only preserved in the ethnographic collections of European museums.[20] Whereas town-dwellers and the upper classes in the countryside shared, through travel, service overseas or illustrated books, in the cosmopolitan fashions of European cities, peasant costumes continued down to recent times to reflect strictly local traditions (Figure 32).

The message that artefacts mirror and reinforce social identity is conveyed most clearly in works of art independent of narrow economic or ecological constraints. Few manifestations speak more directly than the sculptural representations of men and women produced and cherished by the tribal societies studied by ethnographers and it is not to be wondered at that few areas of the international art market have experienced a more rapid appreciation. Working for the most part in the tractable material of wood the sculptors were free to produce representations which whether realistic or not, conformed to the self-image prevailing in their own society. No visitor to a well stocked museum of ethnography can easily fail to be impressed by the marked differences in style of sculptures as between such territories as New Guinea, Oceania, the northwest coast of Canada or various parts of sub-Saharan Africa. The testimony of Henry Moore who once told us that the British Museum served for him as his university is

Figure 31 Maori man with tatooed face, feather head-dress, hair comb, nephrite pendant and nephrite *hei-tiki*. Drawn by Sidney Parkinson on Captain Cook's first voyage in 1770.

particularly impressive on this point.[21] Although on his many visits to the ethnographic galleries he detected 'a common world language of form . . . the same shapes and form relationships', he was no less struck by the 'inexhaustible wealth and variety of sculptural achievement (Negro, Oceanic Islands, and North and South America) . . .' As Raymond Firth long ago impressed on us, the arts of tribal peoples had a strongly social character.[22] The symbolic element in much of the art embodied values common to the society in and for which it was created. The artist worked on traditional themes and expressed common values. In so doing he enhanced the cohesion and self-confidence of the communities in which he worked. Some allowance needs to be made when interpreting tribal art for the physiological and facial differences of different races. That this was not the whole or even a significant element is however evident from the wide range of diversity displayed by the products of Negro sculptors working in sub-Saharan Africa. Partly no doubt because of the fascination they are known to have exerted over European artists of the early twentieth

Figure 32 Men's clothing on Sjaelland during the eighteenth century.
left Bridegroom's clothing from the beginning of the eighteenth century.
centre Bridegroom's clothing from the later half of the eighteenth centry.
right Young man's clothing from Ebberup from 1820–30.

century the masks and figures carved by tribal craftsmen have received close attention from professional ethnographers as well as arousing wide interest among the general public. The range of diversity displayed by these carvings may be appreciated by reference to the illustrations in William Fagg's *Tribes and Forms in African Art*,[23] written in the aftermath of the exhibition shown in Berlin and Paris in 1964. Although the works were chosen from only 122 out of many hundreds of tribal groups, the impressive claim is made that each sculpture could only have been made in a single tribe from the whole continent. It is evident that the sculptors are trained to work in styles traditional to particular tribes (Figure 33). As Fagg expressed it: 'The tribe is an exclusive "in-group", which uses art among many other means to express its internal solidarity and self-sufficiency and conversely its difference from all others'.

How these societies were constituted in such a way that they operated successfully and maintained their forms over periods of time is a topic of vital importance in its own right. It was precisely in the fact that they were structured to ensure the performance and transmission of distinctive patterns of behaviour that human societies have been found to differ most profoundly from those constituted by animals. Breeding and the duties and obligations of individuals in relation to other members of the community were determined in human societies by rules and conventions rather than mere dominance. Meyer Fortes has indeed defined a human society 'as a system of interconnected institutions that regulate social relations and embody norms of right and duty'.[24] There is no need to accept the view which almost seems to colour the writings of some of the more socially orientated anthropologists that men live in order to classify their kin, in order to be able to appreciate the functional value of social structure and the practical importance of the designating relationships verbally. In a way social structure and its recognition played a role in traditional societies akin to that of the vertebrate skeleton: it not only held the body together but enabled it to function in an efficient manner. The context of social structure in the overall cultural heritage has been much debated by professional anthropologists. The truth probably lies with those who admit that it is an independent variable on its own account, but that it accommodates in varying measure to economic and even ecological circumstances. In any case it is common ground that social rules governing the eligibility of mates and the rights and obligations of individual members of communities vary widely in different communities. As it happens some of the most complex social systems observed by ethnographers existed among Australian aborigines

Figure 33 West African tribal masks carved from wood. 1 Bacham tribe.
2 Anyang tribe.

whose material attributes and possessions were among the most
meagre found among men.

The findings of ethnography have confirmed, amplified and greatly
enriched those derived from the fossil evidence of archaeology. At the
elementary economic level communities, equipped with technologies
which might at first sight appear pitiful, managed not merely to adapt
by cultural means to environments so marginal and relatively unattractive that they escaped the cupidity of modern man down to
recent times, but to support varied forms of traditional life and to
experience cultural satisfactions which only the skills of trained
anthropologists are now beginning fully to reveal. Every community
of men was found when first encountered by ethnographers to be fully
articulate. Each possessed a language sufficiently developed to
categorize its enviroment in terms appropriate to its way of life while
at the same time being capable of expressing precise relationships
between different members of the community and generally of facilitating the conduct of social life. Moreover the languages spoken by the
peoples encountered by ethnographers served a further vital need.
Ethnographers have been wise, if they were fully to enter into the lives
of the peoples they studied, to learn the particular language or dialect
concerned. In many ways this was by far the most important cultural
attribute inherited by virtue of belonging to particular groups defined

by history. Language more intensely than anything else combined the roles of enhancing the cohesion and solidarity of human communities and of defining them from neighbours. Another basic contribution of articulate speech was to free men from the brutish limitations of present time. Every human group known to ethnology shares some awareness of the past in however elementary a degree. A sense of history, be it no more than a consciousness of ancestral doings, not merely set men apart from other animals but played a key role in enhancing and validating a sense of separate corporate identity and at the same time helped to generate confidence in building for the future.

Speech and the capacity for thought, so amply displayed by so-called 'primitive peoples', between them did more than facilitate the day to day working of human societies or even free their members as human beings from imprisonment in present time. It made it possible for men to formulate ultimate questions, to ask themselves about the meaning of life and the implications of death. Above all it made it possible and indeed unavoidable to speculate on the nature of the forces which informed and lay behind the outward and visible world. The supreme anxiety of men, and one shared at varying levels by every traditional community known to ethnology, was how to apprehend the hidden forces animating nature, human society and individual persons. The capacity to imagine gods is man's crowning accomplishment, one that in a sense subsumes all the most important qualities that distinguish him from other primates, let alone lower forms of life. Once again, though, ethnographers find themselves confronted by no generalized phenomena. The religions practised by the various peoples they have studied were integral parts of particular traditional cultures. In traditional societies religion was not a separate or distinct compartment of life so much as something that informed and gave meaning and coherence to social life as a whole. This is liable to create difficulties for observers coming from societies in which religion is treated as occupying a sphere distinct from other compartments of life. When the ethnographer Richard Gould sought to define the religious element in the aboriginal societies of the west central desert of Australia he was to begin with at a loss. It was only gradually that he came to appreciate that in aboriginal society religion

> is not a thing by itself, but an inseparable part of a whole that encompasses every aspect of daily life, every individual, and every time – past, present and future. It is nothing less than the theme of existence, and as such constitutes one of the most sophisticated and unique religious and philosophical systems known to man.[25]

Modern anthropologists have made it abundantly clear in countless monographs that religious beliefs and rituals form integral parts of the societies entertaining and practising them. It is even the case as Richard Gould found with his Australian aborigines that religious ideas encompass relationships with the physical environment itself. To the Australians familiar landmarks

> are nothing less than the bodies of totemic beings, or themes connected with them, transformed during the dreamtime into individual waterholes, trees, sandhills, ridges and other physiographic features.[26]

When the aborigines painted rock-surfaces they did so primarily to maintain the harmony between men, animals and the universe which they held to be the essential basis of a secure life. The Bushmen of South Africa had the same idea in mind according to Erik Holm when they depicted their creator in the form

> of an insect or an eland, or the sky, or, again, the stars which they interpreted as dead animals or people awaiting reincarnation.[27]

The execution of rock art is a reminder that religion was never limited to subscribing to a system of beliefs. It always involved social action or conspicuous abstention from certain social activities. The harmony between social life and unseen forces which it was the principal object of religion to promote could only be achieved through the correct performance of customary rites and ceremonies.

If the area of the unknown was in fact more extensive among peoples with elementary technology and a restricted range of knowledge, appreciation of its awesomeness was more intense among communities with a more sophisticated awareness of the precarious nature of their existence. The preoccupation of the ancient Maya[28] with the procession of time or of the Egyptians with the continuity of the dynasties[29] can be matched in more recent times by the concern of the Chinese for the equilibrium not merely of the Empire but of the very cosmos. Over and above local cults designed to guarantee the inhabitants of particular territories against all manner of evil reigned the Official Cult observed by and presided over by the Emperor himself. The fundamental nature of the anxiety that beset the Chinese is sufficiently indicated by the following quotation from Gernet's study of life under the Sung dynasty:

> Religious life seems to have been dominated by a sort of latent and unexpressed obsession: that of the possibility of cosmic disorder. . . . The aim of most religious acts was either to regulate space, to

Figure 34 Australian aboriginal art. Spirit figures and
X-ray fish painted on a rock in the Alligator Rivers
region of Arnhem Land. The art has been preserved by
being frequently retouched by the hereditary owners.

> keep it literally in place . . .; or to regulate Time, inaugurate it,
> renew it – and the annual system of festivals helped to ensure its
> constant renewal.[30]

As for the Official Cult addressed to Heaven, Earth, and the imperial
ancestors, a cult ritually ceremonious, formalistic in detail, grandiose
and colourful,

> its purpose was to ensure the continuity of the dynasty, to regulate
> Time and Space, and to give the world prosperity and peace.

By allaying anxiety and validating social values and institutions
religious observance contributed in no uncertain manner to the
maintenance of social life and entities, quite apart from its therapeutic
value to the individual. Its adaptive value is such that it is small wonder
that ethnographers no less than historians should have found it a
universal phenomenon of social life. By the same token it is no wonder
that the undermining of indigenous religion resulting from contact
with the west has proved as lethal to the survival of cultures as
infectious diseases have unquestionably been in respect of the biological populations that once supported them.

By concentrating on the way in which societies operate while eschewing speculation about how they have come to be what they are, social anthropologists have notably advanced understanding of societies of all periods and places. Yet it is easy to see why anthropologists of a progressive turn of mind such as Edmund Leach[31] and archaeologists and historians of every outlook should find a purely synchronic approach inadequate. The past after all is a record and the future an expectation of change. The societies function as systems but these change in time. Societies observed by ethnographers only appeared to be in equilibrium. In reality they were dynamic. The subdivision of labour to take only one instance generates further subdivision. The greater the benefit it brings by turning out better products for less work, the more likely it is to be intensified. Conversely the more effective specialization becomes, the greater the need to redistribute its products. This in turn enhanced the value of centralized authority for the effective working of society. The emergence of chieftains or their equivalent was one way of ensuring this. To be fully effective leaders needed to define and enhance their superior status by means of insignia and privileges and this in turn increased the prestige which enabled them to stimulate the production of wealth. One way of intensifying prestige, as Thorstein Veblen rather bitterly remarked in a work[32] that might well serve as a text for the higher advertising, was to combine abstention from physical chores with a conspicuous consumption of other men's labour and the most costly materials.

As Peter Bellwood has recently reminded us,[33] paramount chieftains in the Pacific left striking memorials, notably in the scale of temple structures, in the magnificence of war canoes or even, in the case of Hawaii, in the splendour of the feather cloaks and helmets of their regalia (Figure 34). It is easy to understand the impression made on Joseph Banks by the amount of labour lavished on the construction of the great *marae* or temples on Tahiti encountered for the first time by white men on the first of Captain Cook's voyages. Significantly the example that moved him most on the score of size was constructed on the orders of a chieftainess at the peak of her power. Raymond Firth's study of the economics of the New Zealand Maori[34] suggests that paramount chiefs played a prominent and highly advantageous role (Figure 35). One of their main functions was to accumulate wealth, mainly in the form of ornaments, fine garments and stores of food-stuffs and in due course to redistribute this in the form of hospitality and presents. In this way they won prestige both by acquiring riches and by dispensing them. The prestige of chiefs was highly advantageous. It made it possible to maintain a ranking order without the use of force, to initiate new projects, act as trustees for the tribal heirlooms and lands and in this way to enhance group solidarity, control the food-stores that served as reserves and take the lead when engaged in conflict with other groups. On the other hand it should be stressed that the Maori stopped far short of forming anything like modern states and that their societies were by no means rigidly hierarchical. Paramount chiefs were socially pre-eminent and disposed of superior *mana*, but lesser ones graded into the commonalty to whom they were related by blood and slaves were in the main recruited from prisoners of war.

Figure 35 Chief's feather cloak, Hawaiian Islands.

Figure 36 Wood carving
of a Maori chief holding a
symbol of authority in
the form of an adze with a
greenstone blade.

6
High culture in hierarchical societies

Hierarchy and social inequality were not merely the invariable accompaniment but the formative factor in the emergence of high cultures. And by high cultures I mean those whose upper classes observed, or failed to observe, canons of behaviour furthest removed from those of the lower animals.

GRAHAME CLARK[1]

The communities which developed and sustained a variety of high civilizations at different times during the course of the last 5000 years differed fundamentally in structure from those discussed in the last two chapters. They were hierarchical in character, organized on the basis of classes rather than segmentary and based primarily on kinship. They were no longer egalitarian. During the immensely long pre-class phase, in the course of which successive species of men emerged and with almost unimaginable slowness laid the foundations of a progress-ively more human way of life, men lived in small communities as members of groups constituted by genealogical descent. By contrast relations between members of class societies were determined by their ranking in the hierarchies of organizations ranging from city states to theocracies and realms of imperial status. This did not mean that men were freer in egalitarian societies. The contrary might be argued. Even if in real life individuals endowed with exceptional skills, qualities of mind or physical prowess might be granted special influence, men born into societies based on kinship were permanently caught in a web of familial and clan obligations and relationships. Hierarchical societies were as a rule far more open to talent. The need to fill posts in a multiplicity of formally defined grades offered continuing scope for social mobility. Hereditary succession so far from being the rule was exceptional and in the main confined to cases where it in fact offered the most viable solution. In respect of monarchy the hereditary principle offered the readiest solution to the recurrent problem of ensuring a legitimate succession. Similarly, hereditary ownership was arguably the best way of ensuring that land was managed in the long-term interests of the community. Hierarchically constituted societies in fact owed their adaptive advantage precisely to their ability to make the most effective use of their ablest citizens, something hardly to be ensured on a hereditary basis. The initiation of examina-tions as a way of recruiting officials under the Han emperors and its standardization under the Tang did more to ensure the stability and continuity of China than any other act of statecraft.

Some form of ranking exists in all societies, animal as well as human. The role of dominance or ranking order has attracted the attention of ethologists among other reasons because of its adaptive value in the process of evolution. It owes this to the way it promoted genetic competition favourable to the species while at the same time helping to ensure the avoidance of damaging and potentially lethal conflict. As Zuckerman was the first to point out many years ago[2] and as many have since confirmed,[3] patterns of behaviour based on dominance promoted the survival of effective qualities by controlling access to food, breeding territory and mates. When food was short individuals lowest in the ranking order would be automatically excluded.[4] Simi-larly low ranking would exclude less dominant males from access to females. If the effect of dominance hierarchy was to ensure that the genes of the more potent males were those transmitted to future generations, one of its beauties, emphasized by Konrad Lorenz,[5] is that it was normally established and maintained by means of threat rather than open conflict. Physiological signals, including gestures, facial expressions, sounds of menace, violent changes of colour, the emission of smells or at most playful bites, as a rule sufficed.

Two observations by ethologists are worth mentioning for their bearing on human society. The first is that individuals might retain a high ranking long after they had passed their peak for actual conflict if they possessed other attributes important for the survival of the species. For example in the case of some animals the ability to recognize predatory enemies, a requirement for survival if ever there was one, was not innate but one that could only be learned through experience. Among the jackdaws observed by Lorenz the older birds were more valuable to the group by reason of their experience than younger ones and because of this retained a ranking order superior to one they could have maintained through mere physical strength. Lorenz's generalization that 'longevity far beyond the age of reproductive capacity has considerable species-preserving value' has evident and extremely important implications for man. The extension of the human life span far beyond the age of reproduction and well into the period of declining physical strength (Figure 37), a process already advanced in the case of Neanderthal man to the point at which some 3 per cent of individuals were surviving into their fifth decade[6] calls for a similar explanation, with the qualification that in human society the experience of successive generations is accumulated and encoded in the cultural heritage. The transmission of this growing body of inherited experience became a major and ever increasing factor in social life. It progressively extended the period of dependence of the young, reinforced the need for a stable social structure and enhanced the role of the elders. The invention of writing and of subsequent improved methods of data storage and retrieval may have diminished the role of the elderly as the sole repositories of traditional culture in modern society. On the other hand by no means did it impair their functions in interpreting, organizing and evaluating past experience. Still less did it undermine their symbolic role as custodians of ancestral lore and embodiments of wisdom. The fact that thanks to language the cultural deposit is cumulative, despite local disconformities, only serves to emphasize the burden and also the importance of assimilating and transmitting it for the benefit of future generations.

Another insight for which we are indebted to ethology stems from the observation that among Primates a close link existed between learning and ranking order. In his study of the Yale laboratory colony of chimpanzees, R.M. Yerkes[7] noted that these animals 'copy only higher-ranking members of their species'. Similar observations

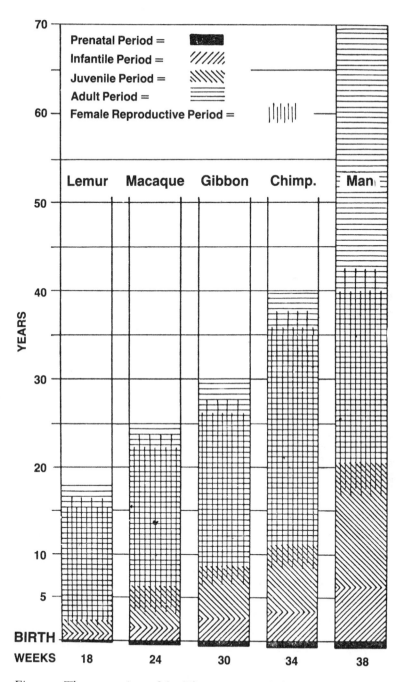

Figure 37 The expansion of the lifespan among Primates. Note especially the extension of adult life beyond the female reproductive period in the case of man.

have been made on the behaviour of Japanese macaque monkeys. Noting the rapid way in which the habit of wheat-eating spread among a colony in the Minoo Valley, near Osaka, M. Yamada[8] attributed this to the fact that it had been introduced by the leader. The suggestion that the spread of new habits among apes and monkeys may be related to gradients passing from dominant to subordinate individuals suggests another reason why dominance appears to have been of adaptive value among animals, since rapid learning was clearly beneficial to the group. This has an evident application to human society.[9] It accords with the observations of ethnographers and art historians that fashions, for example in clothing or furniture, are most commonly devolved from more advanced to less advanced societies and within these from higher-ranking to the lower-ranking classes: for instance the styles of the crudely made but highly coloured furniture made from inexpensive timbers found in Swedish peasant houses throughout much of the nineteenth century were derived immediately from more sophisticated pieces in provincial manor houses. These in turn aped styles introduced to the great houses and royal palaces of Sweden from Germany, styles which originally stemmed from Renaissance Italy. The linked processes of diffusion and devolution that were so amply documented in the later history of Europe and many other parts of the world find their readiest explanation in terms of gradients of social ranking. One might indeed go further and point to the crucial value of these processes in enriching the cultural heritage of human societies as further indications of the adaptive value of the social hierarchy which alone made them possible.

The background to the emergence of polities headed by semi-divine rulers and structured by well defined hierarchies has invariably been a period of sedentary life founded on effective farming. Settled life based on agriculture was conducive to greater differences in wealth than prevailed in societies based on hunting and foraging, notably through variations in fertility, in the availability of raw materials and not the least in geographical situation. The mere fact of permanent settlement magnified the possibility of accumulating possessions. It was only on such a base that sufficient numbers of people could live permanently together in communities large enough for more than an elementary degree of full-time specialization with its attendant network of redistribution to be economically viable. In such a context the need arose for a hierarchy not only of classes but of settlements, with major centres developing as seats of advanced specialization and markets through which products and services could be exchanged to meet the needs of surrounding settlements engaged primarily in the production of food and primary materials. Economic development had important implications for the political ordering of societies. When territories united by economic systems based on the interchange of highly specialized products and services had passed a certain threshold of size, complexity and wealth, there came a pressing need for administrative expertise and above all for the ultimate sanction of force, internally to ensure the smooth operation of increasingly complex systems in the face of individual and sectional cupidity and externally to protect territory, accumulated wealth and access to distant materials against aggressors or rivals. In a word the formation of states was necessitated not merely by the need to protect private property against the envy of the less successful, but far more to promote the public interest. The ultimate sanction of force behind hierarchically organized human societies was in practice for the most part held in abeyance in much the same way as it was in animal societies based on dominance. The day to day running of increasingly intricate systems, the human agents of which, let it always be remembered, were and still are activated by appetites inherited from their animal ancestors, depended on responses issuing from peculiarly human levels of consciousness. In human societies the effective exercise of power has always depended in the long run on acceptance and to be accepted authority needs to be perceived as legitimate.

Among the most effective ways of legitimizing rulers practised since hierarchical societies first emerged has been the attribution to them of divine status. In this way a ruler is automatically endowed with a full plenitude of power extending not merely over social and political activities but even over the natural forces controlling the successful raising of crops and increase of herds. The growth of public religion as against domestic cults, witnessed by the earliest historical records and frequently displayed in the physical structures revealed by archaeology, involved the emergence of priests alongside the administrators, scribes and warriors to whom rulers delegated their authority over particular fields. Equally it was as a rule accompanied by monumental structures which served as symbols legitimizing the state as well as providing facilities for the practice of cults. The prescriptive virtue of time was also called into play, whether in the form of customary or commonly ritualized behaviour or in that of history. The maintenance of dynastic records, the encoding of custom in the form of laws and not least the enacting of rituals in daily life as much as on special occasions helped to endow the existing order of society with the sanction of the past and indeed with sanctity. Nor should the role of symbolism be overlooked. The very monuments that served as temples or as palaces or tombs of the great brought the loyalties of populations to focus on the integrity of their societies and nourished self-confidence at times when the basis of society was becoming more artificial and precarious and men were conscious of depending for very sustenance not merely on the vagaries of farming but above all on an uninterrupted distribution of food. Doubtless also there was a powerful symbolic element in the preparations made to cope with external enemies: defensive works must have served to give reassurance as much as to deter and if necessary afford physical protection from actual attack: and much the same applied to the common practice of endowing rulers with the attributes and panoply of military leadership. If hierarchy was to be fully effective its structure needed symbolic expression. This was achieved in part by regulating the display appropriate to individuals in the lower ranks by means of sumptuary rules but more positively by labelling the higher ranks by conspicuous insignia. Material embodiments of rank took many forms in the diverse civilizations of antiquity. Among the commonest to be preserved in the archaeological record were personal jewellery, weapons, armour and appurtenances, such as horse-trappings or chariots and their gear, of the personal mobility needed even for the display of symbolic leadership in warfare. Such insignia were not merely conspicuous but in very fact embodied power over productive forces. The objects marking off the higher ranks of hierarchical societies were commonly made from the most precious materials and were shaped by the most accomplished craftsmen. Indeed it was precisely in the service of hierarchy that the most splendid works made by the hand of man, works which attract the wonder of those who throng the great museums of our contemporary world, were produced.

A feature conveniently common to the societies of antiquity that attained statehood in the Old World is that they were sufficiently literate to leave behind historical as well as archaeological documents. The role of literacy in such societies should not be exaggerated. It was as a rule limited to particular classes, notably to priests and scribes – not even kings could so much as sign their names in Norman England. Again, it is worth remembering that in the New World a polity as complex as that of the Inca of Peru was capable of functioning without it. On the other hand literacy unquestionably served as a useful if specialized tool in societies where it was current, most notably in the spheres of administration, law and religion and not least for maintaining the dynastic records that helped to sustain the legitimacy of rulers and the stability of states. A feature of early writing of particular relevance to the theme of this book is the range of diversity it displays.

Even a glance at the scripts used in the early writing of Egypt, Mesopotamia, the Aegean, the Indus Valley or north China should be enough to make the point (Figure 38).[10] The materials on which inscriptions were placed and the techniques by which they were applied were also subject to wide variation. In a word writing quite as much as language, art styles or the form of objects in daily use served to symbolize differences and proclaim the identities of human groups. Together with these and other aspects and attributes of culture differences in writing help to reinforce Henri Frankfort's contention that each of the ancient civilizations had its peculiar form. Although he held that the character of civilizations is elusive he was nevertheless willing to follow anthropologists like Malinowski and Ruth Benedict to the extent of recognizing in each

> a certain coherence among its various manifestations, a certain consistency in its orientation, a certain cultural 'style' which shapes its political and its judicial institutions, its art as well as its literature, its religion as well as its morals.[11]

Although he recognized that civilizations underwent changes in time – as an archaeologist he could hardly do otherwise – Frankfort held firmly to the view that what he termed the form of a civilization was indestructible. Civilizations like the smaller cultural units from which they sprang continued to exhibit patterns of diversity. It is true that areas of cultural homogeneity were extended with the growth of larger and more powerful political units. On the other hand this was more than offset by the intensification of cultural identity that went with the heightened tempo of cultural life in hierarchical societies.

The first of the ancient civilizations to receive detailed study was that of dynastic Egypt and partly for this reason we have rather fuller information about its immediate antecedents and the precise context

Figure 38 The diversity of early scripts. Pictographic and historic signs for ox, earth and heaven devised in 1 Assyria and 2 China.

of its emergence.[12] The rich materials excavated from successive phases (Nakada I and II) of the Predynastic period dating from the fourth millennium BC allow one to follow the progress of material well-being from the humble phase of Neolithic farming documented in the Fayum depression. Technical innovations like the use, though not yet the smelting, of copper, the shaping of vessels from hard stone, the crude glazing of steatite beads and the manufacture of more refined pottery, including black-topped ware and the storage vessels with wavy handles that continued to be made during the Early Dynastic age, mark a steady process of technological advance. Change in the political and social sphere appears by contrast to have been sudden. Carvings on a group of stone maces and a slate palette from Hierakonpolis have been widely interpreted as celebrating the unification of Upper and Lower Egypt by force. The scenes on either face of the palette are particularly suggestive (Figure 39). King Narmer, identified by his rebus and almost certainly to be equated with Menes the legendary unifier of Egypt and initiator of the Dynastic period, is depicted on one surface wearing the white crown of Upper and on the other, the red crown of Lower Egypt. The king, shown barefoot and followed by his sandal-bearer, appears in each case as the vanquisher of enemies, viewing decapitated victims or in the act of clubbing a kneeling figure. In addition to appearing as the unifier of his country, Narmer is shown as endowed with the attributes of divinity. He is depicted at larger than human scale and on one face is closely linked with a representation of the falcon-deity Horus with which rulers of the Dynastic period continued to be identified in life.

The land of Egypt was potentially rich in food, due to the sun, the annual inundation of the Nile and the rich red earth deposited as silt, as well as being provided with nearly all the raw materials needed for buildings and crafts. Although the cemeteries of the Predynastic period to some extent reflect this wealth, the full potential was not released until loose confederations of village communities were knit together to form a single realm. One of the more obvious benefits to stem from the unification of Upper and Lower Egypt was the unobstructed use of the Nile for transport. This was aided by the prevailing north wind which pushed sailing craft upstream without being strong enough to counteract the current downstream. The importance of the Nile as an avenue for transport was enhanced by the mere formation of a unified state, one of the principal roles of which was to foster redistribution. Moreover the dynastic and hierarchical nature of the state during the Old Kingdom was in itself a spur to economic activity, notably in respect of monumental building and the

Figure 39 The slate palette of Narmer symbolizing the unification of the land of Egypt which inaugurated the Dynastic era. The king is shown on this face wearing the crown of Upper Egypt. On the other he wears that of Lower Egypt.

manufacture of objects for conspicuous consumption and display. Equatorial Africa was tapped for ivory, ostrich eggs and feathers, gold and a variety of wild animals, Nubia for amethyst and gold, the eastern desert for copper and gold, the neighbourhood of the Red Sea coast for lead, Cyprus for copper and Afghanistan for lapis lazuli. Not the least use made of the Nile was to float the stone blocks quarried on the east side as close as possible to the building sites on the desert plateau west of the river.

Easy generalizations about Dynastic Egypt are peculiarly out of place when one recalls that it spanned some three millennia. In the course of this time the country underwent many vicissitudes. Periods of great achievement and stability, like the Old, Middle and New Kingdoms, were interrupted by interludes during which the very unity of the state foundered and dynasties overlapped or even ran parallel in time. The best way to understand how the system worked is to view it during one of its more successful periods. Contemporary evidence is first available for the later history of the Old Kingdom covering the IV–VIth dynasties. This suggests that the divine kings ruled over the land as though it was their private estate. All its resources, including the human population were at their disposal. In practice effective rule depended on delegating administrative and specialist functions to relatives and trusted officials, who together formed the upper levels of a hierarchically structured system. The people as a whole, who continued to live much as they had done in prehistoric times, found identity and fulfilment in work, in domestic affairs and in vicarious participation in the glittering pageant staged by the king and the various grades in the official hierarchy.

The circumstance that the most prominent archaeological monuments of the Dynastic age are tombs and their contents by no means implies that the ancient Egyptians were morbidly inclined. On the contrary[13] they were so much in love with the good things of this life that they went to exceptional lengths to ensure their continuance in the life hereafter. To accomplish this they took the precaution of mummifying the body to ensure its survival, providing it with food and treasured possessions, enclosing the burial as a whole in a tomb designed to be secure against robbery and not least inscribing the owner's name together with scenes realistic enough to ensure by magic due supplies of food, drink and other goods. It was precisely because they were intended for such a practical purpose that the tomb paintings provide such valuable insights into the economic activities and social ordering of Egyptian life. Despite all precautions the very wealth of the burials of people of high standing ensured that they have rarely escaped tomb robbers. When royal burials did by any chance survive with a reasonable part of their treasures intact they provide a vivid insight into the way wealth was concentrated at the apex of ancient Egyptian society. The craftsmanship shown in the grave goods remaining in the tomb of Tutankhamun who died as a mere youth towards the end of the New Kingdom (XVIIIth dynasty) is sufficiently widely known if only from illustrations. The wealth represented by his burial may be judged from the single fact that his coffin alone incorporated upwards of 300 lbs of gold. Even more striking than the actual burials as evidence for the concentration of expenditure in the hands of rulers and the uppermost levels of society are the monumental tombs and their associated structures. The three pyramids of Giza[14] remain to this day among the most famous buildings erected by man, yet they were raised around four and a half millennia ago by men lacking iron or even bronze tools and equipped with only the most elementary devices to assist human muscle. Moreover they served as tombs for three rulers two of whom, Cheops and Chephren

Figure 40 King Chephren of Egypt and the Horus falcon, Giza.

(Figure 40), were notoriously wicked and tyrannical. Before construction of a pyramid could begin the rock platform had first to be cleared of its overlying sand and gravel and then dressed so that the perimeter of each monument rested on a flat surface. In the case of the Great Pyramid of Cheops the work was carried out so precisely that the surface varied from a true plane by little more than half an inch. The blocks which in this particular pyramid numbered some 2,300,000 weighing on the average about 2½ tons each, had first to be quarried, ferried across the Nile and then dragged by sheer manpower over dry land. The number of unskilled workers required during these preliminary stages has been estimated as of the order of 100,000, supposedly agricultural workers levied at the season of inundation when work in the fields was out of question and the Nile was at its widest. In addition it is supposed that a permanent work force of around 4000 skilled masons would have been needed to dress and fit the stone blocks. How accurately they worked may be judged from the fact that the Great Pyramid deviated only some 7.9 inches from a square each side of which exceeded 9,000 inches, that the monument was orientated remarkably closely on the cardinal points and not least that the blocks of the outer casing were so accurately jointed that they left gaps as little as 0.01 inches in width. If the scale of the pyramids aptly symbolized the power and dominion of the kings, the precision with which they were constructed testifies to the efficiency of their ministers in planning and supervising the work down to the finest detail. The burial of a king in a chamber of his pyramid was by no means the end of his obsequies. His funerary cult was endowed for the rest of time and a mortuary temple constructed to accommodate the necessary priests (Figure 41). Further, a royal pyramid attracted tombs of other members of the royal family, nobles and high officials, so that even in his tomb the king would be surrounded by high-ranking members of the hierarchy. The ordinary Egyptian who worked under the supervision of the bureaucracy on the other hand continued to be buried in the simple manner of his prehistoric forbears.

The form of the civilization that arose in south Mesopotamia differed profoundly from that of ancient Egypt.[15] The inhabitants of the two regions had to come to terms with quite different habitats. The well-being of Egypt focused on the umbilical cord of the Nile, a river whose annual inundation was nothing if not predictable. Further the Egyptians had only to secure a narrow front against Asia to rest secure from enemies of comparable strength. The Nile Valley was insulated on either flank by desert and to the south the peoples of equatorial Africa were relatively undeveloped. If security was a

Figure 41 The Pyramid of Chephren, Giza, Egypt with mortuary chapel in the foreground.

keynote of Egyptian life, anxiety was never far away for the early inhabitants of south Mesopotamia or Sumer. By nature the land was liable to sudden and potentially damaging floods. A combination of exceptionally high tides in the Persian Gulf with the melting of heavy snowfall in Armenia or heavy rainfall further south on the Zagros, not to mention the possibility of landslides in some of the narrower gorges, posed potentially lethal threats. Noah's Flood was only one of many for which there is stratigraphic evidence like the deposit of clay which overlies the earliest traces of human settlement at Ur. Again dwellers on the alluvial plain of Sumer were open to attack from highlanders from the north and east and desert dwellers from the west. The danger from floods was present from the beginning in Sumer. Added to this was the need to build irrigation channels if crops were to be raised in a region with too little rain for dry farming and burdened with the need to keep channels clear of the heavy loads of silt brought down from the north. No wonder that in addition to domestic cults there was a strong emphasis on public worship. Cities and their surrounding lands and not least the people themselves were conceived of as being under the ownership and consequently the protection of the gods (Figure 42). To begin with authority focused solely on temple communities and their priests. Already during the al'Ubaid phase of

Figure 42 Sumerian cylinder seal impression showing a mythological scene with in the middle Shamash the sun god rising flanked on one side by Ishtar and on the other by Ea with fish and water.

settlement temples were being constructed and many times rebuilt. At Abu Shahrain, the ancient Eridu, remains of a succession of no less than eighteen temple structures were found beneath an unfinished ziggurat or sacred mountain. To begin with the plan was that of a simple rectangle, but already in the upper part of the Eridu sequence the traditional form of a central cell with smaller rooms on either side had emerged. The succeeding Uruk phase, marked by monochrome pottery turned on a slow wheel and the appearance of cylinder seals, saw the construction of the 70 metre long White Temple, a white-washed mud-brick structure set on a platform or ziggurat 13 metres high. A vivid impression of what such a sacred mountain or ziggurat must have looked like can be seen from Leonard Woolley's reconstruction of that dating from the IIIrd dynasty at Ur (Figure 43). A further advance in sophistication appeared in the decoration of the Pillar Temple from the overlying Protoliterate level. Hundreds of thousands of coloured clay studs were plugged into the plaster wall of the platform and the free-standing pillars of the portico made of palm stems coated with bitumen were inset by a mosaic of pink limestone, shell and mother of pearl.

At precisely this juncture the first evidence of writing appeared in the form of small clay tablets impressed with signs (Figure 44). The inscriptions turned out to be of a highly practical nature, accounts relating to the operation of the temple estates and stores. So far from

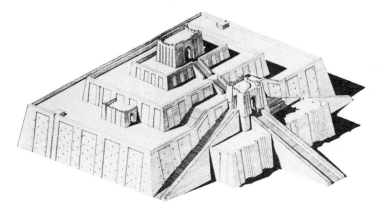

Figure 43 Reconstruction of Sumerian Ziggurat at Ur dating from the IIIrd dynasty (after Leonard Woolley).

Figure 44 An inscribed clay tablet of the Uruk period from Warka (no. 20274.15), Iraq, dating from the late fourth millennium B C and recording a receipt for livestock.

reflecting priestly exploitation of oppressed workers, these accounts relate to collective enterprises in which the economic and religious concerns of the community were combined. If the political unit was the city, the lives of the citizens were largely controlled by the temple communities to which they belonged. Part of the citizen's labour was dedicated directly to the service of his god, that is to working the common land of the temple estate making use of communal equipment, seed and livestock. To maintain his family a man worked an allotment assigned by the temple authorities to whom he paid a proportion of the proceeds in rent. In return for subservience the citizen obtained security. His religious anxieties were resolved by the activities of the priests to whose maintenance he contributed. Equally his economic worries were relieved by the thought of the reserves of equipment, seed and if need be food accumulated in temple stores like those revealed, together with workshops and a priest's house, in the oval walled enclosure of the Early Dynastic temple of Sin at Khafajah. The role of the temple organizations during the earlier phases of Sumerian city life is a reminder that royal power was by no means the only key to high civilization. Traces of kingly identity first appeared in the form of the royal palace at Kish as a structure distinct from the temple complex during the Early Dynastic II phase. The first documentary evidence referring to king and priest as separate persons implying a clear distinction between church and state dates from Early Dynastic III. Present evidence suggests that the appearance of royal authority was a secondary feature in Sumerian life, even if in time it became highly important.

The emergence of kingship and palace organization alongside the temple organization can be interpreted as a response to the second anxiety to overhang the people of Sumer, the need for defence against human enemies. Increasing material well-being brought a corresponding need for defence against predatory enemies and rivals. Every advance in technology and in the need to engage in the conspicuous display involved in maintaining hierarchies underlined the need to ensure supplies of essential materials like metals that were absent from the riverine zone of south Mesopotamia. This in turn involved the backing of military force to ensure access to regions that were often remote. Leadership in war thus became an increasingly important requirement. Although the relationship between the organizations based on palace and temple are not clearly defined for the early period and probably varied widely, it appears that together with their functions as war-leader and law-giver kings were responsible for maintaining a propitious relationship between heaven and earth, whether as intermediary or even as themselves gods.

The manner in which even the petty kings of Sumerian cities distanced themselves from their subjects was vividly illustrated when Leonard Woolley excavated the royal cemetery at Ur dating from the Early Dynastic III period.[16] Commoners, though presumably of the official class, were buried simply, wrapped in matting or enclosed in wooden or clay coffins, at the foot of deep shafts dug, almost invariably in vain, to elude tomb-robbers. The dead, often with

drinking vessel of pottery, copper or stone held to the lip by hands
brought up to the face, were accompanied by personal possessions and
further offerings might be placed in the space remaining at the foot of
the shaft. The royal tombs, also at the foot of shafts, were approached
by ramps to admit the funeral cortège. The tombs themselves were
built of limestone blocks and bricks, kiln-dried as well as sun-dried,
and incorporated such architectural refinements as arched doorways
and vaulted roofs. The superior status of the royal family was defined
both in the wealth of their grave goods and in the ritual observed in
their burial. The finds from the royal tombs at Ur have been described
and illustrated too often to need repetition. It may be sufficient to
recall that they displayed wealth in respect as much of the materials
used as of the specialized skills by which they were shaped. Gold was
lavished on a variety of bowls, goblets and lamps, as well as on
jewellery and conspicuous personal accoutrements such as daggers
and scabbards (Figure 45), silver on vessels and sculptures and semi-
precious stones, including lapis lazuli from the Pamirs, for inlay and
jewellery. Bronze-casters, gold and silver smiths, lapidaries and makers of musical instruments were only some of the craftsmen enlisted to
equip the dead for the next world. The most striking feature of the
burial ritual was the degree of human sacrifice it involved. The king
went to the next world accompanied not only by his women, personal
attendants and musicians, but also by his funeral cortège including

Figure 45 Gold dagger with lapis lazuli handle and decorated gold sheath
from the Royal Cemetery at Ur.

two four-wheeled waggons and their three-ox teams, together with their drivers and attendants and even the armed men at the head of the procession (Figure 46). At what stage in the proceedings, and how the servitors, no less than fifty-nine in one tomb, were despatched is unknown. The fact that the practice of sacrificing retainers on the occasion of royal burials was not carried on in later periods of Mesopotamian history has been explained in terms of economy or even a decline in royal authority. Yet it does not need the exercise of

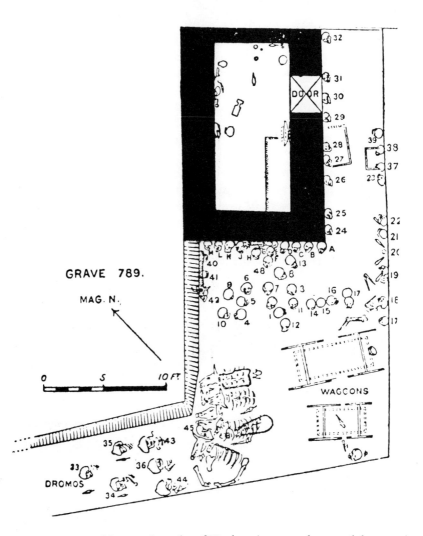

Figure 46 One of the royal tombs of Ur showing attendants and the funeral cortège in the ante-chamber and ramp.

power to maintain practices however burdensome to individuals so long as these are customary features of functioning systems. No one need suppose that the labour for building and rebuilding temples, palaces and dikes or the conduct of the king's wars had to be exacted by royal authority or that their cost was nicely calculated. These services had to be performed if the system was to keep going. A possible explanation for the lapse of this particular practice is that like the waggons used in the procession it was an exotic practice derived ultimately from Inner Asia and never incorporated fully into the form of Mesopotamian society. The relatively common use of lapis lazuli from the Pamirs is evidence that contact however indirect was maintained between the two regions.

As the centre of political power in Mesopotamia moved north from Sumer to Akkad and finally Assyria, the authority of kings and their palace organizations increased. The fact that Assyria was mistress of southwest Asia from the reign of Sargon (722–05 BC) to the fall of Nineveh in 612 BC was due to the exceptional ability of the Sargonid kings and the effectiveness of their institutions.[17] Apart from his active leadership of an efficient and ruthless army, the king fulfilled a crucial role as a divinity as well as representing his people in the conduct of sacrifices and rituals intended to ensure fertility. He disposed of all land, acted as head of the legal system, was responsible for public works, including the building and clearance of irrigation dikes and the construction of roads, and paid close attention to foreign relations, overseas trade and the acquisition of essential materials. In implementing his policy he necessarily relied upon a body of officials from governors of provinces downwards. These were recruited from the upper class of freemen, but as in Tsarist Russia individuals owed their status to their rank in the official hierarchy. Below the freemen the numerous class of workers included a variety of artificers and craftsmen and the large body of agricultural workers on which the system depended for food. At the very bottom of the social pyramid the more onerous work was carried out by a slave class recruited from debtors and the prisoners of war acquired in the course of victorious campaigns. Like all intelligent dynasts the Assyrian kings were well aware that the ultimate base of their authority rested not on force so much as on customary acceptance resting on the sanctions of history and religion. In addition to discharging priestly functions, the kings were careful to maintain libraries and act as the patrons of literature. No one appreciated more than the Sargonids the importance of architecture and monumental art as symbols of their might, majesty, dominion and power. Nor did they overlook the importance of posterity. Their triumphs were duly chronicled in inscriptions graven on stone that men of later ages might read.

The Assyrian kings each in his turn laid out, built and adorned their capital cities very much as the kings of Egypt had chosen the sites and presided over the construction of their own tombs. The scale on which they operated is and was intended to be a measure of their power. If the mud-brick walls of Nimrud enclosed a square mile, including an acropolis containing temples, palaces and the dwellings of high officials some 60 acres in area, the walls of Nineveh as rebuilt by Sennacherib defended a space 2½ miles long and about a mile wide. When Layard quarried into the site he found part of the royal library of inscribed tablets and nearly 2 miles of sculptured stone reliefs, depicting such scenes as triumphs in war, the reception of foreign envoys and kings at their leisure, hunting or feasting. Although much of the heaviest labour was supposedly carried out by slave-gangs, large numbers of skilled masons and stone-carvers would have been needed to embellish structures that were both numerous and large – Ashur-bani-pal's palace alone covered some 6½ acres. The furnishing of these great buildings in a style calculated to symbolize the status of those who occupied them must have called into being veritable schools of artificers working in a great variety of media. One of the more charming recoveries by archaeology, contrasting with the monumentality of the buildings and the frequent brutality of the reliefs, are the delicately carved ivories from Nimrud, comprising among other things component parts of sophisticated furniture, cosmetic boxes, handles of fans and fly-whisks, chariot and horse trappings and a variety of personal adornments.

Chinese civilization[18] developed an individual form differing markedly from those displayed by Egypt, Mesopotamia or for that matter the Aegean or the Indus Valley. Although in the course of four millennia the Chinese acquired some elements of culture from outside – the chariots that appeared in the later Shang period are a case in point – the form of their civilization was unquestionably a native artefact. At the level of material culture the archaeological record shows a steady accretion of the traits that went to characterize Chinese civilization. Jade, which still exerts an almost mystical fascination for the Chinese, was already being worked in Neolithic times in the form of pebbles of nephrite obtained from the region of Lake Baikal or even from Inner Asia. Despite the fact that it is harder than steel the prehistoric Chinese were already working it into axe blades, knives and personal ornaments, but significantly also into the flat discs (*bi*) and square-sectioned blocks with tubular sockets and lateral grooves (*zong*) symbolizing heaven and earth. During the Shang and Zhou dynasties jade began to be used for funerary purposes being buried in contact with the corpse and serving to close the orifices of the body. By the Han dynasty it was being celebrated by scholars as the fairest of stones and endowed with the five virtues of charity, rectitude, wisdom, courage and equity. Furthermore the use of iron tools in conjunction with hard abrasives made it possible to produce three-dimensional figures, as well as the ornaments, belts, hooks, seals and other furniture for the scholar's desk in which men of a certain standing now deemed it appropriate to indulge. Jade is indeed an outstanding embodiment of the persistence of a civilization's form. The working of jade reached its peak during the first half of the reign of Qianling (1736–96) (Figure 47). Jade is still worked, though in degenerate style, and is often faked or copied in softer stones.

Painting by means of hair brushes, which underlay the calligraphic and pictorial arts so highly esteemed under later dynasties, was probably a refinement of the craftsman's skill in painting decorative

Figure 47 The technical climax of jade carving from the Qianling period. The ovoid vase together with its lid attached by a chain has been carved from a single block of pale greenish-white nephrite.

designs on pottery, already well displayed on Neolithic Yang-shao ware. Instances have been cited of oracle inscriptions of the later Shang dynasty applied by means of a brush and certain graphs from this time have been held to represent books in the form of bundles of bamboo slips of the kind on which inscriptions were customarily painted. Such slips are known from late Zhou times and an actual hair brush has been recovered from a tomb of the third or fourth century BC. The earliest evidence for pictorial paintings comprise silk fragments from the Late Zhou dynasty and representations on the walls of tombs of the Han dynasty. Silk, one of the Chinese inventions for which the world has most reason to be grateful, was certainly being made during the Shang dynasty and there are hints that another Chinese contribution, lacquer, was being applied to tombs from the same time. By the later Zhou dynasty lacquer-work was already an established craft and from it was made a wide range of objects including cups and bowls, toilet boxes, shields, scabbards and wall-paintings. Porcelain, defined as a hard translucent ware fused at a high temperature, did not finally emerge until the Tang dynasty when it soon established itself as the finest of all ceramic wares.

Archaeology has also thrown significant light on the emergence of the Chinese polity which so intrigued the philosophers of the French Enlightenment while themselves engaged in undermining traditional culture in western Europe. Excavation has uncovered settlements and cemeteries of the Shang (traditionally Yin), the earlier phase of which (c. 1650–1300 BC) documents the initial stage in the process of achieving statehood. At Zhangzhou traces have been found of a centre covering over 3 square kilometres, which probably served as a focus of a ruler's power with space for his chief supporters as well as for his own palace. The surrounding wall of compressed earth was c. 20 metres wide at the base and perhaps 10 high when built, a structure variously estimated to have required the labour of 10,000 men for between 12½ and 20 years. Rectangular platforms for wooden buildings, some of large size, found in the interior stand in marked contrast to the semi-subterranean cabins of the Neolithic peasants and point to a more advanced society with a hierarchical rather than an egalitarian structure. For the later Shang period (c. 1300–1027 BC) the documentation furnished by the excavations in the neighbourhood of Anyang is notably more complete. Here large living structures are complemented by cemeteries which include shaft-graves approached by ramps for the burial of royal personages and others of high rank. High status is suggested among other ways by evidence for the sacrifice of human beings both to accompany the dead and to inaugurate the construction of palace buildings. Whether or not this implies the existence of a slave class as Marxist archaeologists have claimed or whether the victims were prisoners of war, their sacrifice is a sure indication of social stratification. The burial of chariots with great men (Figure 48) and the provision of sumptuous weapons suggests that formalized warfare was an institution and argues for endemic fighting between petty kings, chieftains and their retainers. Confirmation that this was indeed so has come from decipherment of the questions inscribed on oracle bones recovered from the same locality.

The appearance of writing in the context of achieving statehood was common to all the early civilizations so far explored in the Old World. On the other hand the script devised by the Chinese was distinctive. Despite a continuing process of reformation it is significant that between 30 and 40 per cent of the signs employed during the later Shang dynasty have their equivalents in modern Chinese. It is not for

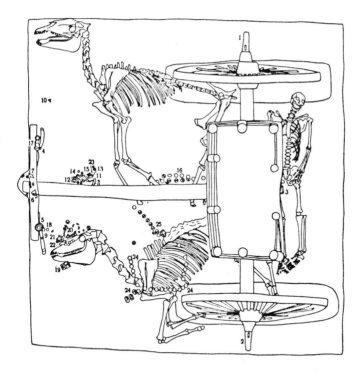

Figure 48 Plan of a late Shang dynasty chariot burial from Anyang. The charioteer lies across the back of the box and the pair of horses with traces of harness either side of the shafts.

nothing that the Chinese people continue to employ a script that has served them well over more than three millennia, has entered deeply into their aesthetic and at the same time so visibly proclaims their identity as bearers of one of the most distinctive civilizations of mankind. The practice of inscribing questions on animal bones and tortoise shells and seeking answers from the course taken by cracks induced by the application of heat, apart from preserving the earliest evidence for Chinese writing (Figure 49), has thrown important light on the nature of later Shang society beyond what could be learned from architecture and material culture. The practice of scapulomancy played an important part in Shang statecraft. By asking key questions and obtaining answers in advance, Shang rulers and their subordinates invested their decisions with oracular authority while avoiding direct responsibility in the case of misadventure. As well as furthering economic and military affairs, scapulomancy helped to ensure that relations between the ruler and his ancestors were kept on an auspicious footing, a crucial prop of his own legitimacy. This by no means lessened the need for the appropriate ritual, though it may well have made it more effective. Certainly in the case of rulers and members of upper levels in the hierarchy ancestors were worshipped in a ceremonial fashion with priests and the service of bronze vessels of

Figure 49 Fragment of Shang dynasty oracle bone inscribed with a divination about hunting.

traditional form and elaborate decoration. The vessels employed in the ceremonial of ancestor worship during the later Shang and the Zhou dynasties (c. 1030–221 BC) were cast in elaborate ceramic moulds and have been widely acclaimed as among the finest bronzes ever made (Figure 50). Inferences from oracle bone inscriptions backed up by the excavation of actual workshops suggest that the subdivision of labour had already been carried to a relatively advanced stage among craftsmen under the Shang rulers. In addition to bronze-smiths, there is evidence for specialists in working bone and stone, as well as potters, sculptors, chariot-builders, weapon makers and many another group of artificers whose finest products were already serving to define and enhance the effectiveness of the still incipient hierarchy of the Chinese state.

If Chinese civilization was substantially an indigenous growth one might expect to find Shang sites concentrated in the heart of the zone previously occupied by the pioneers of settled life in China. This is precisely what we do find. Indeed the main weight of Shang settlement coincided with the area of overlap between the two Neolithic cultures of north China, the Yangshao and the Longshan. The southward extension of the frontier to the Yangtze was accomplished under the Eastern Zhou, a period that saw the expansion of agriculture, a growth in the number of cities and an increase in the scale of political units and warfare. The process of unifying the Chinese state was advanced under the Qin dynasty by standardizing weights, measures and coinage, organizing the army on a national basis and incorporating local boundary defences into the Great Wall, but it was under the Han dynasty (206 BC–AD 222) that China expanded to its historic boundaries and became a veritable empire. The enlargement of territory and continuing growth in the complexity as well as in the scale of the economy had major implications for Chinese society. Above all it called for an administrative machine manned by officials of higher uniform standard than a hereditary system could ensure. Under the Han dynasty the hereditary nature of official posts was abolished except for a limited number of kings and marquises. Ability and achievement were accepted as a basis for recruitment to the bureaucracy of what was now an extensive empire. Competitive examinations were used at first only to a limited extent to grade recruits nominated for the public service. Under the Tang emperors examinations had become the main avenue for recruitment. By the Song they were recognized as an institution of paramount importance if the state was to fulfil its perceived objective of providing good government by good men upholding good doctrines. What European philosophers of

Figure 50 Shang bronze casket of *fang-i* type decorated with masks and dragons. One of the many types of vessel used in the performance of ritual associated with ancestor worship.

the eighteenth century admired was the success of the Chinese in maintaining what we should call the form of their civilization despite the irruption of barbarians and political upheavals, while continuing to dispense good government with the minimum of overt compulsion. All this was achieved without religion appearing to form a significant part of the structure of the state. It would be wrong to think that the Chinese were lacking in religious sentiment. It is true that Buddhism from its entry under the Han dynasty never assumed the importance as an organization which it attained in India or southeast Asia. Yet popular religious sentiment certainly entered into the rituals practised in connection with the sacrifices and ancestor worship encouraged by Confucian scholars.

The moral order that enabled the Chinese state to prosper and survive with so little direct intervention depended on deep-seated philosophical concepts. The key to behaviour was held to lie in maintaining harmonious relations between the individual, society and the natural world. Confucius and his followers stressed the need for men to behave in a manner appropriate to their status in society. Only in this way could they expect to find satisfaction in playing the parts allotted to them in the social hierarchy and only so could personal contentment be reconciled with the stability of the state. Confucian teaching was reinforced by historical sentiment. Chinese scholar-officials, themselves selected for their proficiency in the classics, were well aware of the value of history as a stabilizing force. For this reason they encouraged the long-established practice of ancestor worship as a way of integrating kinship groups and legitimizing existing institutions. At the highest level court historians were maintained to ensure that a correct version of history was recorded and transmitted, when necessary by expunging errors from earlier records. In society at large the past exerted its beneficent influence primarily through ritual observances associated with sacrifices and ancestor worship but also with the transaction of official business from the imperial court downwards. Michael Sullivan has maintained that as far back as the Zhou dynasty the court had become 'the focus of an elaborate ritual in which music, art, literature and pageantry all combined under the direction of the master of ceremonies (*pin-hsing*) to give moral and aesthetic dignity to the concept of the state.'[19]

The principle of *li* or propriety propounded by the philosopher Mencius during the late fourth century BC was embodied in a social hierarchy which in turn determined through patronage the kind of art and handicrafts produced. Whereas in modern societies the tone has come to be set by men selected by their success in acquiring and accumulating money, in imperial China taste was controlled by those of high official status, from the emperor downwards. Sullivan wrote[20] of the art of the Song dynasty that it 'was produced by, and for, a social and intellectual élite more cultivated than at any other period in Chinese history. The pottery and porcelains made for their use is a natural reflection of their taste.' Regardless of personal wealth members of the official class were guaranteed a style of life appropriate to their status.[21] Sumptuary laws were frequently enacted to close certain avenues of conspicuous consumption to men of lower ranks. It follows that the finest products were made for the use of the imperial family (Figure 51). The most highly prized porcelains and stoneware in the world today are those produced in the imperial factories for the exclusive use of the Song emperors. Although the imperial court topped the system of patronage that elicited the superb products of Chinese taste, it was one of the strengths of Chinese civilization that it was widely diffused in the provinces. Garrison towns in remote areas might be significant centres of patronage. There scholar-officials and local gentry sought to live lives of cultivation. In doing so they gave employment to the artificers who congregated in the towns for

Figure 51 Stoneware bowl-stand of the Northern Song dynasty with the crackled greyish-blue glaze of *ru* ware.

their service. The connection between local patronage and the production of fine things has been well brought out by Hsiao-Tung Fei:

> The greater the concentration of landowners as well as wealth, the greater the development of craftsmen and the more skilled and varied the types of things they produced. The silver of Chengtu, the embroidery of Soochow, the silk of Hangchow, and the cloisonné of Peking are all examples of art handicrafts which attained a high degree of development. [22]

Great importance was attached to defining the various levels in the hierarchy. Many grades were recognized within the official class and signalized by meticulously defined entitlements in respect of the ornaments applied to garments. Within the class of commoners precedence was given to scholars not of the official class, but still graded as men who worked by their brains. Farmers were placed next since they were deemed the most productive of those occupied by physical labour and were followed by artisans and merchants. The low ranking of merchants shows how little mere wealth ranked in Chinese society. Although in daily life merchants undoubtedly fared better than petty traders and shop-keepers, even the richest had been legally excluded from wearing silk or using horses since Han times. Below the various ranks of commoners, whose children could rise to the official class if bright enough to score well in the examinations, was the class of mean people – slaves, prostitutes, entertainers and government runners – who since they were excluded from intermarriage with members of higher classes had small chance of upward movement in the hierarchy.

A leading concern of the Chinese was to maintain harmony between opposites. Safety was thought to reside in the opposition of the complementary cosmic forces Yin and Yang, forces which needed one another to exist and whose opposition could only be disturbed at the risk of disaster. The drive to social conformity and the emphasis on harmony between man and society that flowed from the teachings of Confucius was matched by Lao Tzu's emphasis on the need to relate to nature by submission regardless of all else to the universal *tao*. Only so could men resolve the apparent opposition of spirit and matter. This was a main reason for the primacy of painting among the arts in China. Its practice and contemplation brought men into a closer relation with *tao*. Before putting a brush to paper the artist studied nature in all its aspects. His painting was not an outcome of mere visual confrontation. It was a distillation of accumulated experience and understanding, a veritable fragment of eternity. If the painter omitted shadow and ignored perspective he did so in order to escape from the limitations of the particular and penetrate to the essence of things. By painting on scrolls and leaving vacant spaces in the composition rather than seeking to fill a well-defined frame the Chinese artist showed that his works were not intended as definitive, so much as invitations to explore. As the official paused in his labours and unwound his scroll he sought refreshment for his spirit and renewed contact with the *tao* by taking imaginary journeys in the landscapes it depicted. Alternatively he might contemplate the embodiment of the Tao, the dragon itself, all pervasive but only to be captured by an artist sufficiently skilled to represent it (Figure 52). A clear sign of the high prestige of painting is the interest displayed by the emperor and the official class in collecting, patronizing and frequently in practising the art. Despite the threat to his frontiers the last of the northern Song emperors Hui-tsung (1101–25 AD) found time not only to practise painting and calligraphy at a high level of proficiency (Figure 53) but also to supervise his court painters so closely that he would set them themes, often a line of poetry, and in less happy vein would dismiss those who stepped too far out of line. One of the main sources of the vitality of the art is that it was widely practised and collected by scholar officials often far away from the capital. The close association of painting with the court and the governing class, like the nature of the official examinations and the rituals used in the transaction of public business, goes to emphasize the

Figure 52 Part of a scroll depicting nine dragons by the Song painter Ch'en Jung (active 1235–*c.*1260).

strong aesthetic element not merely in Chinese civilization but in the Chinese state.

It is appropriate to end this chapter by commenting, even if only impressionistically, on some aspects of European civilization as this developed since the passing of the Classical world. Europe after all has given rise to the most brilliant, but also the last of the great traditional civilizations. At the same time it provided the seed-bed and forcing house of our present era, one in which the basic concepts informing traditional civilizations have been condemned as obsolete and their products relegated to auction-rooms, museums or the works of archaeologists and art historians. Piquancy is added by the reflection that the original proponents of the Enlightenment that undermined the old regime and helped to usher in the new were themselves distinguished ornaments of the most brilliant European society as well as being self-confessed admirers of the celestial empire of Qi'an Long.

From prehistoric times and notably from the Later Stone Age onwards the cultural history of the European peoples has been marked by outstanding diversity and dynamism. Geographical and historical

Figure 53 Painting of a five-coloured parakeet on a silk handscroll by the Song Emperor Hui-tsung.

circumstances have each been favourable. Ecologically Europe spans three major zones of climate, vegetation and animal life, as well as comprising marked differences in relief and including a tract of Atlantic seaboard from Africa to well north of the Arctic zone and a significant part of the Mediterranean basin. Geographically the continent lay open to the east to contact with the extensive and varied territories of Eurasia, but also to the south with North Africa and the southeast with southwest Asia. To these avenues of potential cultural enrichment the great voyages of discovery, which as much as anything signalled the end of the Middle Ages, added the New World, southeast Asia, the Far East, Australasia and the Pacific. Last and most important there were significant variations in historical antecedents. Even the prehistoric heritage, the only one common to the continent as a whole, was already patterned by cultural diversity of the kind discerned by prehistoric archaeologists. The experience of classical civilization common to the Mediterranean and the Balkans, was only shared by the western half of the north temperate zone, and within the frontiers of the Roman Empire varied greatly in depth and character. Although politically Greece became subject to Rome it never lost its cultural or spiritual identity, a fact that has continued to influence the course of history down to our own day.

Parts of temperate Europe had been incorporated as provinces of the Roman Empire, but it is substantially true that the territories north of the Alps as well as those east of the Carpathians were civilized by the medieval church. Although sundered by the schism between the Catholic west and the Orthodox east, Christendom disposed of a formidable strength. Between the passing of the Roman imperial system and the rise of dominant lay hierarchies in the form of cities and national states, the church was able to concentrate a sizeable proportion of the wealth of a substantial part of Europe in the service of a single overriding idea. Almost everything worth another glance made in Christendom between AD *c.* 800 and 1400 stemmed from the direct patronage of the church, a rigid hierarchy organized on the basis of function rather than birth. Jean Renoir, son of the painter and himself a distinguished film director, hit the nail squarely on the head in his correspondence: 'If Christianity had triumphed in its primitive form, we would have had no cathedrals, or sculpture, or painting.'[23] So long as it combined immense wealth with a monopoly of learning and the disposal of spiritual sanctions which included the power to excommunicate kings and lay their kingdoms under interdict, the church was able to raise buildings to the glory of God that dwarfed the houses of the people and exposed in their crudity the massive castles that housed kings and barons. Furthermore they were able to beautify and refine their buildings and above all to furnish them and enrich their rites with the exquisite works of art that excite the cupidity of the richest men and the wealthiest foundations of the present age. Some, like illuminated manuscripts or in the Byzantine world mosaic work, stem directly from classical sources. Others, of which stained glass windows are a supreme instance, were original contributions to the arts of mankind. Despite its hierarchical structure, the use of a single language for its governance and rites and subscription to a single body of doctrine, the medieval church displayed, most notably in its architecture, a fair measure both of dynamism and regional diversity.

This can also be illustrated by architecture. Like the religion itself Christian architecture stemmed from the Roman world. Byzantine structures in the east, like Romanesque ones in the west as far north as Britain and Scandinavia, were based on the rounded arch and the dome. In the Mediterranean this basically Roman tradition proved remarkably enduring. In the temperate zone on the other hand it underwent a profound change. The Gothic style of the Catholic west, by replacing the rounded by the pointed or ogival arch and the dome by the ribbed vault, made it possible to reduce the mass of masonry and enlarge the area of windows for the display of coloured glass. In the east Orthodox architecture, though clearly deriving from Byzantine sources, underwent marked changes as it spread into forested environments. The influence of timber architecture long established in the region was manifest in the polygonal plans of chapels and the use of pyramidal tent-like roofs. Similarly the onion-shaped profiles of domes and terminals were well adapted to shedding snow, although doubtless elaborated and perpetuated as symbols of Orthodox identity. This by no means exhausts the diversity of Christian church architecture in Europe. Each of the main traditions experienced a variety of regional and temporal styles extending into the present century, including the outcome of hybridization.

The fracturing of Christendom north of the Alps effected by the Reformation marked a permanent shift from a quasi-theocratic to a predominantly lay state of society. The dominant institutions were no longer the church but national states, principalities and urban oligarchies, but hierarchy continued to prevail as a principle of social organization. The outcome of concentrating patronage was displayed most extravagantly in the royal palaces of the kings of France at a time when they presided over what was unquestionably the most cultivated as well as the most powerful state in Europe. The palace of Versailles in its ornateness and size, the richness of its appointments and its

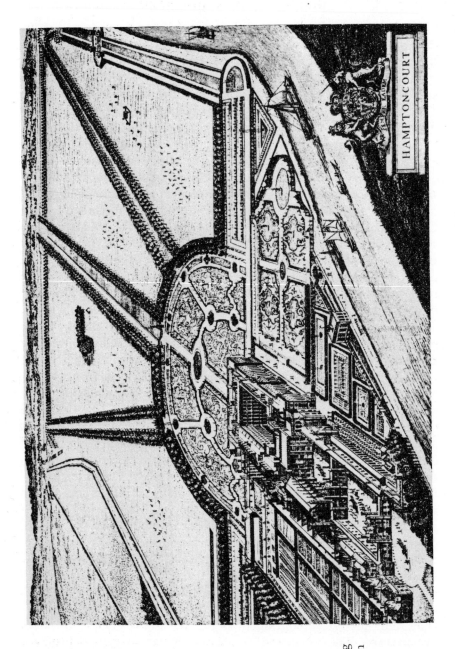

Figure 54
Landscaping
of Hampton
Court
Palace
under
William
and Mary.

domination of the landscape aptly symbolized the crowning situation of Louis XIV at the apex of the glittering and formidable pyramid of the French state. Similar evidence of dominance, though on an appropriately diminishing scale, was exhibited at the courts of lesser monarchs (Figure 54) and princelings and in the graded hierarchy of seats of provincial magnates, each in his varying degree diffusing rays of civilization from the sun king over his bucolic neighbours. In such a society every man however humble had his appointed place and shared even if vicariously in the most advanced civilization. Judged by modern standards the gross national output of French agriculture, industry and commerce during the seventeenth and eighteenth centuries was pitifully small. Yet by keeping consumption vicarious above subsistence level for the majority and concentrating it in the upper levels of the social hierarchy in a manner only exceeded by the medieval church, a modest productive base was capable of supporting one of the richest cultures of human history. If the furniture and silverware made for the French or foreign courts is too ornate for modern bourgeois taste (Figure 55), the level of technical achievement and the harmony of styles it represents are regarded by specialists as the highest in their

Figure 55 Silver gilt tureen from the Paris Service made for Catherine the Great by François-Thomas Germain (1726–91).

fields attained by men of any period or culture, as outstanding in their way as the *ru* porcelains of the Song dynasty of China. This is only one illustration of the general theme that the finest material embodiments of the human spirit were the products of societies in which spending power was concentrated in the fewest hands. Even more significantly in some respects, it is precisely such objects, the finest in their respective classes, that attract the admiration and wonder of the citizens of modern egalitarian societies reduced to staring in museums and show houses at relics of the great civilizations in which their forbears however vicariously once shared.

7
Homogenization and dehumanization

Perhaps one of the most obvious weaknesses of present-day civilization lies in an inadequate view of man. Without a doubt, our age is the one in which man has been most written and spoken of, the age of the forms of humanism and the age of anthropocentrism. Nevertheless it is paradoxically also the age of man's abasement to previously unsuspected levels, the age of human values trampled on as never before.

JOHN PAUL II[1]

History tells us of innumerable retrogressions. . . but nothing tells us that there is no possibility of much more basic retrogressions than any so far known, including the most basic of them all: the total disappearance of man as man and his silent return to the animal scale.

JOSÉ ORTEGA Y GASSET[2]

The definition of man as a cultured Primate aware of his past and capable of exercising choice in respect of his future has been reached by following differing but converging routes. Ethology has brought out similarities, but more significantly has helped to define the differences in behaviour which separate man from his closest, though still extremely remote, relations. The prime respect in which men differ from the other Primates, let alone from the rest of the animal kingdom, lies in the degree to which their behaviour is patterned by cultural rather than genetic inheritance and not least in the extent to which men are aware of their unique situation and are to that extent free to initiate change. Since abandoning pseudo-historical reconstructions of the supposed evolution of human society and concentrating on how individual societies in fact lived, Anthropology and its descriptive arm, Ethnography, have revealed something of the astonishing diversity of cultural patterns displayed by peoples once stigmatized as primitive, a diversity that stems ultimately from the freedom of choice inherent in the attainment of humanity. Archaeology has and is currently engaged upon complementing the synchronic by a diachronic, dynamic view of human society. Archaeologists are peculiarly well suited for this task because the artefacts which inevitably accompanied the evolution of culturally conditioned behaviour form his particular stock in trade. By studying sequences of artefact assemblages and their associated structures the archaeologist is well equipped to reconstruct the emergence of specifically human patterns of behaviour. It is already possible to conclude that not only the behavioural patterns but even some of the distinctive physical features of man are themselves artefacts. If the emergence of man and his progressive humanization appears to have extended over at least 2 million years the rate of change can be seen to have speeded up dramatically since the appearance of modern man during a comparatively late stage of the Upper Pleistocene. Closely linked with this acceleration in the rate of cultural evolution went a marked intensification in the diversity of cultural patterns culminating in the hierarchically structured civilizations of the historical period.

Archaeology, anthropology and ethology alike point to cultural diversity based on the ability to define values as epitomizing the very process of humanization. By contrast with other animals whose behavioural patterns are determined by their species, are programmed by genetic inheritance and with only minor and local exceptions are homogeneous within breeding populations, it is of the essence of human beings that they conform to the customs and values of the societies to which they belong, societies which being constituted by history are necessarily unique. Men have not attained to human dignity by sharing a generalized culture, nor have they reached their peaks of attainment by achieving the abstract status of being civilized. They have achieved humanity by sharing specific cultures and particular civilizations. The concept of values could only be entertained in terms of specific cultural traditions. As it was well put many years ago, a man can only experience the values of civilization by being 'within the living currents of his own civilization . . . it is only as active participants in the life of a civilization still being enacted that values as such enter into the picture.'[3] The point of view adopted in the present book has been elegantly expressed by the anthropologist Clifford Geertz:

> If we want to discover what man amounts to, we can only find it in what men are: and what men are, above all other things, is various. It is in understanding that variousness – its range, its nature, its basis, and its implications – that we shall come to construct a concept of human nature that, more than a statistical shadow and less than a primitivist dream, has both substance and truth. . . . To be human . . . is thus not to be Everyman; it is to be a particular kind of man.[4]

Complementing diversity between cultures is the range of variability within cultures sufficiently advanced to require vertical as well as horizontal structures. Hierarchical societies were able to make their superlative contributions to human culture to the extent that expenditure and patronage was concentrated at or near the apex of the various civilizations. The finest artefacts of whatever category and the ones that exhibit intercultural diversity in the most pre-eminent degree were the outcome of social inequality and privilege often of the most extreme kind. The humanization of man beyond the modest level of the Lower Palaeolithic was the outcome of diversity and inequality. Between them they created the traditional societies known to archaeologists, ethnographers and historians, including ironically enough those based on western Europe and its outliers that give birth to the world community which threatens to homogenize and dehumanize mankind.

The storming of the Bastille and the execution of Louis XVI and his queen symbolized the end of traditional societies as political institutions, even though the process was not finally completed until during ensuing centuries modern regimes were installed over much of eastern Europe, the Far East and Iberia. As so often happens political changes merely registered in a public way changes already well advanced at more fundamental levels. The transformation of traditional into modern societies stemmed from the revolution in thought embodied in the rise of natural science during the seventeenth century. The notion that it was possible to understand and to that extent control the world by the systematic application of the human intellect supported where necessary by practical experiment without reference to received authority or divine revelation was explosive in its implications. The impact of scientific modes of thought whose wide-ranging impact on culture was signalled by T.S. Eliot and I.A. Richards and advertised by F.R. Leavis[5] rapidly extended far beyond the cultivation of the natural sciences or the transformation in technology and economic life which their success entailed. Their application to human affairs has been as profound as it has been in some respects destructive of the dignity of man. The eighteenth century witnessed the classical expositions of many of the basic ideas of the Enlightenment, notably freedom of thought and expression, the rights and equality of man and the idea of progress, ideas which taken together were incompatible with maintenance of the old order of society. If the revolutions in North America, France and Russia were carried through by tough men resorting when necessary to brute force, they drew their real strength from manipulating ideas generated by philosophers who applied scientific modes of thought to the problems of society. The disciplines of economics and sociology took their modern forms at this time in the hands of men like Adam Smith and Montesquieu. It is furthermore worth recalling that the same period witnessed the formation of archaeology as a disciplined mode of extending the range of history beyond the scope of written documents to embrace mankind at all levels of culture and in every part of the world.

The limitations of the natural sciences in relation to the human sciences have been most clearly perceived by eminent scientists. Professor Victor F. Weisskopf's address on 'Frontiers and Limits of Physical Sciences', which opened the celebration of the Bicentenary of the American Academy of Arts and Sciences in May 1981 may serve as a case in point.[6] Professor Weisskopf began his hierarchy of material systems in time with the big bang and ended it with the emergence of man and a cultural mode of life. He rightly saw that it was the cumulative learning made possible by language that led to 'the formation of autonomous structures within the behaviour patterns of the species' that we term 'cultures and civilizations'. A second point emphasized in his address is that cultural evolution proceeded on a much faster time scale than biological evolution. Thirdly he recognized the part played by individuals in the cultural process, a fact that in itself implied that the human sciences could hardly be predictive in the same sense as physical sciences. Without excluding the possibility of detecting trends or even laws in human affairs, Weisskopf concluded that in dealing with these it was most commonly the case that 'it is the specific that is relevant and not the general'.

The main damage has come from those who fail to appreciate the consequences of Weisskopf's hierarchy and seek to apply modes of thought and procedures developed in the course of understanding and manipulating matter to the enormously greater complexities of human affairs. It is only so long as the fundamental difference between science and the humanities, including the arts, is recognized that fruitful co-operation between the two is feasible. Archaeology is a conspicuous case in point,[7] just as unhappily it offers plenty of scope for the misapplication of scientific concepts and procedures. What then are the essential differences between the two? The short answer that natural scientists deal with matter and humanists with people needs to be qualified from both directions. When scientists concern themselves with men, they do so from a quite different point of view. And the same applies when scholars and artists address themselves to nature. The prime aim of the natural sciences is to discover laws capable of prediction, laws capable of obtaining further insights into natural phenomena or alternatively of being turned to practical use in fields like medicine, military affairs, technology or the production, storage and processing of food. To achieve this the scientist effectively limits himself to what can be counted and measured and concentrates on defining abstract categories. He continually seeks to bring a wider range of phenomena within the scope of fewer and more potent laws. Such laws being abstract are universal if true. They therefore serve both directly and through imitation to promote and render respectable the culturally degrading process of homogenization.

Cultural traditions by their nature reflect diversity and favour historical modes of thought. The arts are concerned more with persons and personal reactions than with things as such, with quality rather than quantity and with diversity and individuality rather than with homogeneous abstract categories. From the standpoint of an archaeologist or historian science being progressive is by that mere fact of only temporal validity, whereas the arts stand aside from progress because they correspond to eternal verities. As Jean Renoir has expressed it in terms particularly apposite to the theme of the present chapter:

> Painters know that material needs are relative, and that the satisfactions of the mind are absolute. Scientists try to balance the two pans

of the scales, loading one pan with more and more material desires and the other with their fulfilment. It is an endless process, in which the pan weighted with desires is always the heavier. With the painter, on the other hand, results are lasting. The satisfaction derived from the Lascaux *graffiti*[*sic*] is equal to that got from a still-life by Braque.[8]

Renoir's final comment reminds one irresistibly of Herbert Read's considered judgement:

Some of the painters of Greek vases, some of the medieval illuminators of manuscripts, the great painters of the Renaissance, certain painters of the nineteenth century – all these have perhaps reached the level of aesthetic quality present in the cave paintings of Lascaux or Altamira, but they have not exceeded that original standard.[9]

In the traditional cultures recovered by archaeology,[10] the products of graphic and sculptural art and architecture mirror cultural diversity with all the greater sensitivity that they are relatively freer from the constraints of utility than the generality of artefacts. The converse is no less true. The graphic and sculptural products of modern society reflect with startling clarity the degree to which the human spirit has already been impoverished by abstraction. In painting the process has taken two main forms but the outcome is essentially the same. At one extreme the artist resorts to elementary geometric forms or covers the whole of his picture with a single colour, as with Malevich's famous white on white series or Rodchenko's riposte in black on black. At the other extreme he depicts natural forms of artefacts with a fidelity that rivals the camera. The effect in either case is to deprive the work of cultural content. Geometry and photography operate, like the laws of natural science or the processes of modern technology, irrespective of cultural endowments. Furthermore, the practitioners of modern abstract art, while striving for originality as innovators as though they were scientists, often seek to eliminate personal as well as cultural diversity, if necessary by using spray guns or applying natural or ready-made materials.

Sculptors have equally sought to evade cultural affiliations or even personal identity. This has sometimes been achieved, as with Paolozzi, by combining parts of machines or, as with Vantongerloo or Caro, by using wire or standard products of machine industry. An alternative has been to adopt and improve upon natural forms such as Brancusi's eggs or Moore's animal bones. In architecture it is much the same. Modern structures recalling factory products betray their indifference to ecology by obtruding alike from Brazilian rain forests or

Arabian deserts and display their contempt for man and his traditions by overshadowing without prejudice oriental mosques and pagodas or the classical, gothic, and neogothic structures of the western world. As eloquent as the nature of its products in some respects is the fact that the very term 'architecture' has been abandoned by some progressives as in itself anachronistic because of discriminating in respect of quality. The substitute term 'built form' serves the dual purpose of advertising the divorce of building from culture and the devaluation of that very discrimination by which men emerged from the other Primates and diverse civilizations developed in the course of ages from the base of primitive communism.

A similar process of homogenization deforms the ideas and concepts that once inspired and embodied the identities of the several civilizations of mankind. This is true most notably of the religions that more than anything inform the arts and enshrine the beliefs of these civilizations. The positivist temper until recently prevalent in natural science undermined traditional beliefs in whatever sphere primarily on the ground that their validity was incapable of proof. Religion of whatever description was regarded as incredible, irrational, and superfluous because all phenomena that were real were held to be susceptible to explanation in terms of natural science. Religious belief indeed could even be condemned on the ground that it impeded the progress of natural science and was therefore not merely obscurantist but positively harmful to the prospects of mankind. If rationalism was hostile to religion in general, it was still more opposed to the notion of diversity of belief. It is of the nature of scientific laws to be universal in their application, whereas beliefs, codes of social behaviour or artistic conventions are by their mere origin particular to historically constituted communities. The universalizing character of natural science has so conditioned modes of thought that even those who retain religious faith find themselves increasingly unable to tolerate religious differences. So far from proclaiming belief in the rightness of their own particular creed, religious leaders proclaim the need for ecumenical thought, not merely as a practical necessity but as desirable on its own account. Religions when not flatly repudiated are increasingly being homogenized not by their enemies but by their friends.

In many ways the most revealing manifestation of popular feeling in societies of collapsed hierarchy is the cult of what Karl Popper aptly termed 'biological naturalism', manifested in diet, the immitigable growth of hair, nudism, sexual permissiveness, and even bestiality. It is encouraging to a prehistorian whose profession leads him to trace the emergence of man from a state of nature, whose subject rests on the assumption that men become human to the extent that they elaborate cultural modes of behaviour to find the following appreciation of the implications of this vulgar heresy by this eminent philosopher:

> It must be admitted that certain forms of behaviour may be described as more 'natural' than other forms, for instance going native or eating only raw food; and some people think that this in itself justifies the choice of these forms. But in this sense it is not natural to interest oneself in art, or science, or even in arguments in favour of naturalism. The choice of conformity with 'nature' as a supreme standard leads to consequences which few will be prepared to face; it does not lead to a more natural form of civilization, but to beastliness.[11]

As Popper wrote later on in the same work, emphasizing his meaning by italicizing the sentence:

> *There is no return to a harmonious state of nature. If we turn back, then we must go the whole way – we must return to the beasts.*[12]

Indeed, the position of lapsed men is in many ways worse, since they have lost the instinctive guides to behaviour on which other animals are able to depend.

At the level of daily life the advance of homogenization has been accelerated and made more effective through economic constraints. The most comprehensive of these has been the incorporation of traditional societies within the nexus of a world-wide market in the products of machine industry. Whereas in preindustrial societies of the kind most commonly encountered in archaeology the elaboration of hierarchy and the enrichment and diversification of culture were adaptive and for that reason selected not merely for survival but for enhancement, in the case of industrial society the precise opposite applies. Standardized products of the kind most readily manufactured by machines, because of their greater cheapness, have a built-in advantage over handmade ones reflecting local skills and the styles of diverse cultural traditions. Economic forces left to themselves increasingly ensure that handmade products displaying regional diversity become too costly for daily use. Outside museums they can only survive as luxuries, but luxuries imply disparities in consumption which industrial societies serve to reduce. The trend towards uniformity applies not merely to different societies but to classes within them. Articles that deviate from the standard become too expensive to buy in the very societies in which it pays to spend the maximum amount in promoting the consumption of standard ones by means of advertising and persuasion in a variety of media.

The price mechanism is powerfully reinforced in this regard by ideology. The 'enlightenment' which generated natural science and in due course modern industrial economies itself seeks to promote equality as a desirable aim of society. Egalitarian notions affect patterns of consumption directly through the impact of steeply progressive taxation, but also indirectly through the psychological constraints. Even the very rich are increasingly inhibited from consuming luxuries they can still afford for fear of appearing conspicuous. In striking contrast to their behaviour in hierarchically structured societies in which status is in a measure defined by conspicuous consumption, in industrial societies they strive to remain inconspicuous and so to avoid even heavier fiscal penalties for their success. Economic, social, political and psychological forces thus combine to maximize the production and consumption of common things while penalizing that of uncommon ones. Indeed, the degree to which the common man dominates consumption has come to be accepted by capitalists and Marxists alike as an index of progress. Societies in which the production of exceptional things is matched by marked inequality in consumption have even come to be accepted as backward. The richer in economic and the more 'progressive' in political terms the world becomes the more relentlessly it is impoverished with respect to the very attributes that mark the emergence and cultural enrichment of mankind.

Another powerful force making for cultural homogenization has been the dramatic advance in systems of communications in the industrial world. Railways, motor vehicles and aircraft have shrunk the world so that formerly remote territories have been brought within effective reach of a single market dominated by a comparatively few states which share a common technology and modes of thought powerfully influenced by the concepts of natural science. The installations and mechanisms that now girdle the earth not merely conform in all essentials to universal patterns but for the most part are themselves manufactured at a few centres. They bear no more relationship to modes of transport traditional in most parts of the world than they do to local ecological systems.

Even more important as a factor in the process of homogenization than the movement of men and goods is the communication of ideas. Printing and the electronic transmission of texts and the spoken word have brought the peoples of the world within range not merely of a single technology and market but even more significantly of concepts linked with the pursuit of economic profit, scientific comprehension, and notions of social injustice. Again, the new facilities have conferred decisive advantages on those able to communicate directly with representatives of the dominant western culture. Just as mass production involved the standardization of goods, so improvements in communication have promoted the domination of progressively fewer languages. Again, as modern business soon appreciated, television is an unrivalled medium for manipulating, standardizing and so making more profitable the satisfaction of consumer tastes. More than that, its effect must be to undermine traditional modes of thought and values. The impact of electronics has been further amplified by computers, which by sorting data from the whole range of science and the humanities has helped still further to break down conceptual barriers while at the same time giving rise to a jargon common to all cultures and disciplines. Inevitably, modern media for the transmission of ideas operate to favour universal as opposed to local patterns of behaviour. In this way they serve to reinforce uniformity at the expense of diversity both within and between communities.

The process of homogenization is already far advanced in most developed countries and strong economic, social and ideological forces are still operating to eliminate the last traces of diversity and inequality. Yet the body of western civilization is not yet cold, even if the main signs of life take the form of protest. Whatever intellectuals and 'progressives' – even the Gadarene swine were making progress – may say, people at large value their heritage, enjoy the complexities of social life, cling to their identity as groups and are determined however confusedly to defend their dignity and integrity as persons against the forces of anonymity and homogenization.

Three main forms of protest may be singled out for comment in western society, those based on generational, occupational and regional concerns. In some respects the strongest and certainly the shrillest protests come from those who at their peak of emotional and intellectual awareness stand at the brink of adult life. It is the young who perceive more sharply than their elders already enmeshed in the system the nature of the sacrifice required of them as persons. The conveyor belt of the consumer society has few attractions at least for the more intelligent. Work, which through past ages engaged the affective emotions of those engaged in it, appears joyless to those invited to become part of an impersonal machine, and the consumer goods which come as compensation may seem distasteful if not degrading. It is no accident that the phenomenon of dropping out is most pronounced in societies which in terms of the materialist ethic have been most successful. Alcoholism, addiction to drugs, withdrawal to Aegean islands, the banks of the Ganges or whatever remote location happens to be in fashion, cultivating grotesque clothing and hair, rejecting conventional patterns of behaviour, and adherence to a strange variety of gurus and cults are only some of the many forms of youth protest. These go far beyond seeking to impress their identity on their seniors. They add up rather to an expression of disgust and dismay. A striking fact about this protest is that it is being made with varying intensity all over the world, although most markedly in societies that like to regard themselves as technologically, but also socially and politically in the vanguard of progress. Only the relatively poor countries of the Third World, understandably anxious to catch up in the race of economic development, have so far been relatively immune. There the young flock to man the new machines and national performance tends to be measured by the extent to which the delights of the consumer society, identified with western culture, are available to populations whose own indigenous cultures had until recently enriched the world. Although more visible in California or Tokyo, not even the repressive powers of state and party have managed to keep the Soviet young uncontaminated by such insignia of youth culture as jeans, pop records or significantly the rites of the Orthodox Church. Plainly the protest goes deeper than politics. It is aimed against a denial of a basic human drive, the creative impulse to shape matter and produce results through the co-ordination of hand, brain and eye, by which as we have argued man in very fact made himself. The Palaeolithic flint-knapper, the Neolithic potter, the Bronze Age metal-smith, the Sumerian or Mycenaean gem-cutter, the Chinese jade carver, the medieval stone mason, the skilled ploughman, reaper or thatcher all in their different ways found fulfilment in their work. As well as acquiring status through the exercise of skill, no one who has examined archaeological or ethnological artefacts can doubt that their makers experienced deep aesthetic satisfaction from turning out work to standards of excellence well beyond what was required from a narrowly functional standpoint.

If those who choose to drop out at least for a spell make a stronger appeal to the media, by far the greater proportion of the young in industrial societies press forward to secure places on the conveyor belt. So strong is the attraction of the consumer society to the unsophisticated that extending the age of compulsory schooling meets the strongest opposition from those it is intended to benefit most. It is precisely here that the system displays its greatest and from one point

of view its most sinister strength. The goods and amenities it pro-
duces, attractively packaged and advertised with all the arts of flattery
and snob-appeal, are so seductive that workers are by and large only
too willing to barter their dignity as human beings to secure their
share. Indeed their only form of protest is by collective action to ask
for more. It says much for Karl Marx's innocence that he imagined a
perpetual state of conflict between workers and owners when in fact
they had an overriding common interest. The only way to sustain
increases in production was to enhance the worker's ability to con-
sume by increasing his wages.

Loss of the emotional satisfactions once experienced by craftsmen in
the course of their work is only part of the story of deprivation. At
least as important, as persistently stressed in the present work, was the
satisfaction to maker and user that came from conforming to specific
cultural patterns. In undermining diversity the process of
homogenization serves to destroy the entities in and through which
men have traditionally achieved and expressed their humanity. Many
of the key issues of contemporary life revolve around the opposition of
the logic of history focused on cultural values and an abstract logic
concerned with economic and social themes. As seen from the standpoint of the present book the opposition could be expressed in more
controversial terms as between those whose prime concern is with the
values which distinguish men from apes, in other words with the
dignity of man, and those prepared to treat men as though they shared
much the same aims as caterpillars. If increasing the consumption of
material goods and ensuring equal rations is the prime aim of society a
likely result is to impoverish life by promoting homogeneity at the
expense of cultural diversity. 'Progressive' opinion is inclined to treat
opposition to this trend as though it was compounded of stupidity and
self-interest, instead of convictions based on the logic of history. The
strength of the cultural roots of such convictions can be seen in the
demands for local autonomy, not infrequently backed by violence, on
the part of groups submerged by some of the most advanced states of
western Europe. Not surprisingly language, the most effective way of
unifying and defining cultural communities, is a common rallying
point for Basques, Bretons and the Celtic speakers of different parts of
the British Isles and Ireland. To animadvert on the divisiveness and
expense of duplicating educational and other services would be to
exhibit a failure to comprehend the supreme value placed on cultural
integrity. The European Economic Community is another case in
point. From an abstract standpoint national frontiers have long
appeared as anomalies, impediments to the free play of the world

market, barriers to intellectual and social intercourse and potential sources of conflict between states. Popular sentiment tends on the other hand to view frontiers as boundaries between communities constituted by sharing different and in some respects conflicting histories and values. Any threat to national frontiers encounters opposition and this is likely to be the more intense the more reasonable it appears to be. Military threats can be relied upon to generate the response elicited by any menace to the integrity of territory. In the case of institutions and changes like those sponsored by the European Common Market the fear is that by administrative stealth and as a rule unintentionally they may serve to undermine traditional ways of doing things. Although in many cases indefensible from a rational point of view, traditional customs and usages may still have a profound value to those whose lives they help to shape. It is beside the point to argue the logical superiority of litres to men accustomed to drink their beer by pints. The process of homogenization, however convenient to administrators and accountants, is one which carried to its conclusion destroys not merely the diversity of cultural patterns but the dignity of man himself.

One of the biggest and most salutory shocks to liberal concern has been encountered in the field of race relations. The long struggle to secure the admission of negroes to white society in the United States was met in the moment of apparent triumph by resistance on the part of young negroes to the idea of assimilation. The notion that blacks would find fulfilment in being accepted as whites was in itself a survival of a mentality fostered by nineteenth-century ethnography and evolutionism. The idea that to differ from western norms was to be primitive led very easily to the notion that admission to western culture was an ultimate aim which people had only been prevented from realizing because of colonial or social repression. Liberation certainly brought economic and social relief, but among those with even a minimum of education it also generated less grateful thoughts. The endeavours of white liberals, missionaries, administrators and business men could no longer be viewed objectively. Instead they were seen as part of an homogenizing process undermining the integrity of diverse cultures and assimilating them to the dominant culture of the benefactors. The depth of feeling behind negro consciousness is illustrated by the institution of black studies programmes in American universities and at a more popular level by the phenomenal success of *Roots*. The attitude of American negroes can be paralleled by less prominent minorities. To the average westerner the provision of financial compensation and social care might be considered a sufficient answer to the grievances of native populations when disturbed by pipelines, mining projects and other economic developments. It is increasingly evident that this is far from meeting the case. What is at stake and what even peoples until lately qualified as 'primitive' increasingly realize to be at stake is nothing less than their integrity as bearers of particular cultures, in a word as human beings. This has recently been well expressed by Mr Justice T.R. Berger of the Supreme Court of British Columbia in his contribution to a seminar held at the Australian Institute of Aboriginal Studies. Justice Berger allowed that land rights and social concerns were prominent in the minds of Canadian Indians and Australian aborigines alike when confronted by modern economic projects, but he was concerned above all to draw attention to

> a third common concern and that is resistance to the concept of assimilation. In both countries it is apparent that there is a fierce desire to retain the defining characteristics of cultural identity.[13]

In the case of Canada the fact that native peoples learned to speak English and adopted many elements of western material culture too often leads the white population to assume that Indians and Eskimos no longer thought of themselves as possessing separate identities. Justice Berger's enquiries showed him that this was far from being the case. He found that the native peoples

> treasure their past; they want their language to survive; they want their traditions to survive – respect for the land and respect for their elders, the idea of making decisions by consensus. They simply do not accept that they should assimilate and become people indistinguishable from the descendants of white Europeans.

The situation in North America has obvious implications for Britain as it faces a comparatively rapid increase in its non-European population. Considerations of public order and a deep-rooted wish to live in a harmonious society have combined to form a climate favouring fair treatment for new citizens wherever they come from. Compassionate feelings as always need to be directed by clear thinking. If human dignity is the highest good and if we are right in thinking that men are artefacts of culture and draw their humanity by virtue of adhering to specific traditions, we have to ask whether cultural homogenization through assimilation is either fair to the new immigrants or in the best interests of the host country. It is a matter of common observation borne out by studies in the classroom, that the immigrants most successful in adjusting and contributing to British society are precisely those who, like the Pakistanis, have been most careful to retain and transmit their own cultural traditions. If over the centuries Britain has been immeasurably enriched by immigrants, this is largely because they brought with them their own special cultural skills and values. Those who have reached the country more recently and from more distant shores also have their contributions to make. This can only happen if they are treated not as statistical abstractions but as human beings, people endowed with cultural traditions and values of their own.

The problem of reconciling economic well-being with the maintenance of cultural identity can be seen in reverse form in territories affected by the intrusion of western technology. Leaders of the new states of Africa, many of them trained in the west, were all of them aware of the expectations of their newly independent citizens. It is no wonder that there was a rush to acquire western technology, raise material standards and acquire at second hand the debased trappings of western consumer society. The rich diversity of indigenous African culture was severely undermined and the world to that extent impoverished. Yet all is not yet lost in Africa. The growing recognition that western technology to be fruitful needs to be appropriate, that is adapted to local ecology and not least to indigenous customs and skills, increases the possibility of making real economic progress in a manner consistent with maintaining cultural values. Nationalism is also working in the same direction. In countries, many of which had little or no written history and much of that dating from the colonial period, indigenous artefacts provide convenient rallying points, a matter for patriotic pride as well as a means of lending colour to the daily scene. The support given to archaeological research, the display of archaeological finds in museums, the conservation of monuments and the use of archaeology as an academic subject has already been remarked (p. 47). The safeguarding and indeed revival of indigenous arts and crafts such as wood-carving and textiles in daily life and not least in schools and institutions of advanced education are another potent means of rebuilding interest in indigenous culture. Symbolic gestures by leaders can also play their part. Kenyatta's fly-whisk may have brought superior smiles to the faces of international newsmen, who were probably unaware that the kings of Assyria at the height of their glory made use of the same device. It is probably no accident that the most successful leader to emerge in post-colonial black Africa was one of those who stood closest to his cultural roots.

Recent events in Iran show what can happen if people realize in time the true nature of the threat posed by the homogenizing power of world economic forces when applied to their own country. The late Shah earned the plaudits of the west for his apparent success in dragging his archaic realm into modernity in record time. All was set fair when the mullahs blew the regime sky-high. The revival of Islam and the power it placed in the hands of the clergy met with some incredulity outside Iran. Men who had lost faith in their own identity found the Iranian reaction to western materialism hard to understand. Yet the crowds who hailed the downfall of the Shah and his regime were not composed of old men clinging to archaic shibboleths but young men reclaiming their heritage, proclaiming their identity as Iranians. What the Iranians have been asserting in however distressing a manner is their dignity as men.

What can be done to arrest the destruction at the hands of homogenization of the few indigenous cultural traditions still surviving in outlying parts of the world? How can unique cultural resources be saved to enrich mankind instead of surviving if at all only in ethnographic monographs or as specimens in museums? Plainly it is too late, even if morally justifiable, to attempt to cocoon the few indigenous peoples left with the substance of their own cultures and preserve them in reserves uncontaminated by contact with the modern world. As we have already seen even the peoples encountered by early ethnographers during the nineteenth century were already to some degree changed by contact with Europeans. Where, as with the Danes in respect of the Greenland Eskimos, a conscious effort was made to shield a native people from external contact, there was always the risk that, as happened during the war of 1939–45, isolation might be rudely broken and find the people ill-equipped to withstand the shock. The only course promising a measure of success in the long term is not to shield so much as to build up the resistance and vitality of native cultures. The first need is to acquire a full, caring and loving understanding of indigenous cultures and their unique sets of values, something which needs to be planned by trained anthropologists but which if it is to prove effective must be shared by the people themselves. It is understandable that when the inhabitants of the New Guinea highlands were encountered during the war still using stone axes and practising prehistoric modes of horticulture, anthropologists and their research students closed in on them very much as biologists converge upon new species in their habitats. Greater sophistication has emphasized the need to involve the people themselves not merely in the interests of science but to further their own future well-being. The urge to describe native cultures before they perished, which impelled Haddon and his pupils to lowland New Guinea, has been supplemented by the realization that by enlisting the people some at least of their values might be conserved. The idea that traditional values might be saved from extinction to serve as arsenals for the cultural activities of future generations has been well expressed in respect of the South Pacific by Axel Steensberg. In his report to UNESCO Steensberg emphasized that the attainment of political and economic independence provided no more than a setting. If the new life was to be worth living native peoples should be able to build on their own cultural traditions and values. In these circumstances Steensberg wrote:

> It is of urgent importance that the cultural heritage of these peoples should be conserved and taken care of so that they can know who they are, what are their roots, how their forefathers lived, for this can provide them with sufficient ballast for survival in a world of increasing standardization according to the European and American pattern.[14]

The trend towards reducing and ultimately eliminating diversity of cultural expression is complemented by a parallel one to flatten social hierarchies. So long as traditional societies prevailed social hierarchy was accepted as a corollary of civilization. One of the crucial challenges to the existing order on the part of the eighteenth-century Enlightenment was Rousseau's claim that men were not by nature free or slaves but equal. The Declaration of the Rights of Man and Citizen of 1789 proclaimed that 'Men are born and remain free and equal in rights. Social differences, therefore, could only be based on general utility.' If men were born equal it seemed reasonable to ask why they were not in fact free. Sociology and the self-torture of middle-class consciences were well and truly launched. The fact remains that inequality is a feature of all civilized societies, though taking a variety of forms. Perfect equality is generally recognized to be unattainable except at a totally unacceptable price, completion of the process of dehumanization. Professor Ralf Dahrendorf's endorsement[15] of Immanuel Kant's pronouncement that 'inequality among men' should be considered a 'rich source of much that is evil, but also of everything that is good' expresses most of what needs saying.

So far as the evil is concerned the application of mechanical power to industry has largely removed the need for the human drudgery involved in creating the structures of traditional civilizations. Similarly the standardization and profusion of modern industry has created a market that can only be absorbed by the producing masses. It is no longer the evils of inequality about which we need to worry so much as the potential outcome of pursuing equality to the point at which the dynamic qualities of inequality are lost to society. As for the good that issues from inequality an attempt has already been made in the previous chapter of this book to illustrate the truth of Kant's concluding remark by reference to the archaeology of hierarchically organized societies.

This does not prevent Marxist propaganda from repeating the ancient myth that only the workers create what is exploited by the upper classes. In the brief foreword to the finely illustrated book,[16] widely distributed in conjunction with the recent exhibition of Chinese art and archaeology shown at centres in the west, the ritual bronze vessels of the Shang dynasty were hailed as demonstrating the 'intelligence and creative ability of the slaves [sic]'. The suits, each made of 2000 or more finely cut jade plates joined by gold wire, in which Prince Liu Sheng of the Western Han dynasty and his wife were buried (Figure 56), each estimated to represent the equivalent of more than ten years' work by a skilled artisan, were held to 'glaringly expose the luxury and decadence of the feudal ruling class, and their inhuman exploitation of the working people'. Everything, it was claimed, went to show the truth of the saying that 'the people, and the people alone, are the motive force in the making of world history' and confirm the claim that 'without the creation by the labouring people there would have been no ancient culture, no history'.

No one who gave more than a passing glance at the exhibits could withhold admiration for the skill and devotion of those who laboured to shape them. In that respect they were creations of their artificers. Yet if these things, or for that matter the jade vessels, silks, porcelains, lacquers and paintings, or indeed the fine products of any high civilization, had not been made for superiors in the social hierarchy they would not have been made at all. If the ruling classes had not been luxurious and sophisticated and if they had not been in a position to enlist the skills of the artificers these things which define and illustrate the essential qualities of Chinese art would never have existed. And the same applies to the treasures of Tutankhamun's tomb or the Sutton Hoo ship burial. Without a hierarchic structure, without a marked degree of inequality in consumption, the astonishing diversity of Chinese, Egyptian or Anglo-Saxon culture would never have developed. This is not a matter of speculation. We know what the culture of China, Egypt, or Britain was like before class societies developed in these lands. Archaeology tells us much about their prehistoric peasant populations. They were relatively egalitarian. They were illiterate. And their material products by comparison with

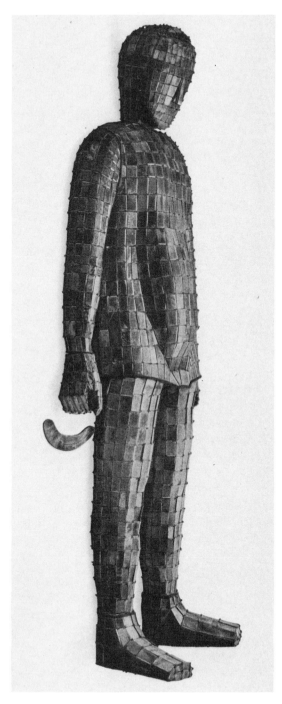

Figure 56 Funeral
garment of
Prince Sheng of
the Western
Han dynasty
composed of
over 2000 jade
plates tied
together with
gold wire.

the fine things produced in the ambience of class societies were as dull as those used by the lower classes in Shang China, Pharaonic Egypt, or Anglo-Saxon England.

The essence of the matter was expressed in his old age by the painter, Renoir, and recorded by his son, Jean:

> It is the art lovers who do the painting. French painting is the work of Monsieur Choquet. And Italian painting is the work of a few Borgias, Medicis and other tyrants who God blessed with a taste for colour.[17]

The degree of inequality implied in the exercise of patronage remains as it always has done an essential ingredient of civilized societies. In more general terms one may agree with Dahrendorf's wide-ranging pronouncement:

> The very existence of social inequality, however, is an impetus towards liberty because it guarantees a society's on-going dynamic, historical quality. The idea of a perfectly egalitarian society is not only unrealistic; it is terrible. Utopia is not the home of free-dom . . . ; it is the home of total terror or absolute boredom.[18]

References

Chapter 1. Introduction

1 Charles Singer, *Technology and History*, L.T. Hobhouse Lecture no. 21 (London 1932), 9.
2 Glyn Daniel (ed.), *Towards a History of Archaeology* (London 1981). Also, the following periodicals: *Antiquity* (Cambridge), *Archaeology* (New York) and *World Archaeology* (London).
3 Grahame Clark, *World Prehistory in New Perspective*, 3rd edn (Cambridge 1977); P.R.S. Morley (ed.), *The Origins of Civilization* (Oxford 1979); Andrew Sherrat (ed.), *The Cambridge Encyclopaedia of Archaeology* (Cambridge 1980).
4 T.E. Allibone, Sir M. Wheeler *et al.* (ed.), *The Impact of the Natural Sciences on Archaeology* (Oxford 1970); Grahame Clark, *World Prehistory and Natural Science*, Det Kongelige Danske Videnskab. Selsk. Hist.-Fil. Kl. 50:1 (Copenhagen 1980).
5 Don Brothwell and Eric Higgs (ed.), *Science in Archaeology*, rev. edn (London 1969); M.S. Tite, *Methods of Physical Examination in*

Archaeology (London 1972). Also the following periodicals: *Archaeometry* (Oxford) and *Journal of Archaeological Science* (London).

6 Grahame Clark, *Archaeology and Society*, 3rd edn (London 1957); David L. Clarke, *Analytical Archaeologist. Collected Papers of David L. Clarke* (New York and London 1979); Mark P. Leone (ed.), *Contemporary Archaeology. A Guide to Theory and Contributions* (Carbondale, Ill. 1972); Colin Renfrew and Kenneth L. Cooke (eds), *Transformations. Mathematical Approaches to Culture Change* (New York and London 1979).

7 R.A. Gould, *Living Archaeology* (Cambridge 1980).

8 J.E. Doran and F.R. Hodson, *Mathematics and Computers in Archaeology* (Edinburgh 1975); Renfrew and Cooke (eds), op.cit.

9 Susan E. Shennan, *Social Organisation in the Earliest Bronze Age in Czechoslovakia: a study based on the cemeteries of the Nitra Group*, Camb. Univ. Lib. Ph.D. Thesis no. 10767 (1978).

10 *Animal Liberation* (London 1976). Reviewed by Myron Ebell, *The Cambridge Review* (5 December 1980), 46.

11 W.H. Thorpe, *Animal Nature and Human Nature* (London 1974), 357–60.

12 Kenneth E. Boulding, 'The human mind as a set of Epistemological Fields', Emory University Symposium, 1979. Cited from *Bulletin of the Am. Acad. of Arts and Sciences* XXXIII, no. 8 (May 1980), 29.

Chapter 2. Men and Primates in fossils and in life

1 Clifford Geertz, *The Interpretation of Cultures. Selected Essays* (New York 1973), 46–9.

2 Bernard Campbell, *Human Evolution* (London 1966); W.E. Le Gros Clark, *The Fossil Evidence for Human Evolution*, 2nd edn (Chicago 1964); *History of the Primates*, 9th edn (London 1965); William Howells, *The Evolution of the Genus Homo* (Reading, Mass. 1973); G. Isaac and E.R. McCown (eds), *Human Evolution: Louis Leakey and the East African Experience* (Menlo Park, Calif. 1976); G.H.R. von Koenigswald (ed.), *Hundert Jahre Neanderthaler* (Cologne 1958); K.P. Oakley, *Frameworks for Dating Fossil Man*, 3rd edn (London 1969).

3 T.H. Huxley, *Evidence as to Man's Place in Nature* (1863).

4 P.V. Tobias, '*Australopithecus, Homo habilis*, tool-using and tool-making', *South African Archaeological Bulletin* XX, no. 80 (1965), 167–92.

5 J. Desmond Clark, 'African Origins of Man the Toolmaker', in

Isaac and McCown (eds), op.cit., 1–52; Glynn Isaac, 'East Africa as a source of fossil evidence for human evolution', ibid., 121–37.

6 C.D. Ovey (ed.), *The Swanscombe Skull*, Roy. Anthrop. Inst. Occ. Paper no. 20 (London 1964).

7 von Koenigswald (ed.), op.cit.

8 Grahame Clark, *World Prehistory in New Perspective*, 3rd edn (Cambridge 1977), 28–9.

9 C.B.M. McBurney, *Early Man in the Soviet Union. The Implications of Some Recent Discoveries*, Reckitt Lecture, British Academy (1976).

10 Desmond Morris, *The Biology of Art* (London 1962).

11 Alexander Marshack, *The Roots of Civilization* (New York 1972).

12 S.L. Washburn (ed.), *Social Life of Early Man* (London 1962).

13 op cit., especially chap. 10.

14 I. DeVore (ed.), *Primate Behaviour. Field Studies of Monkeys and Apes* (New York 1965); A.H. Schultz, *The Life of Primates* (London 1969).

15 S. Zuckerman, *The Social Life of Monkeys and Apes* (London 1932).

16 W.H. Thorpe, *Animal Nature and Human Nature* (London 1974).

17 V.C. Wynne-Edwards, *Animal Dispersion in Relation to Social Behaviour* (Edinburgh 1962).

Chapter 3. Approaches to archaeology

1 Herbert J. Muller, *Uses of the Past* (New York 1954), 441.

2 G.E. Daniel, *The Three Ages. An Essay in Archaeological Method* (Cambridge 1943).

3 Joan Evans, *Time and Chance* (Oxford 1943), 100 f.

4 E. Lartet and H. Christy, *Reliquiae Aquitanicae*, ed. Rupert Jones (1875).

5 G. de Mortillet, *Musée préhistorique* (Paris 1881).

6 *Man Makes Himself* (London 1936), 6.

7 Quoted from M.W. Thompson's Preface to his translation of A.L. Mongait's *Archaeology in the USSR* (Harmondsworth 1961), 20.

8 In his famous lecture on 'The study of kinship systems', *J. Roy. Anthrop. Inst.* LXXI (1941), 16.

9 ibid., 3 and 16.

10 Clyde Kluckhohn, *Anthropology and the Classics* (Providence, RI 1960), 14, 45 and 49.

11 Quoted from an essay originally published in 1966 and reprinted in *The Interpretation of Cultures. Selected Essays* (New York 1973), chap. 2. Geertz believed that anthropologists had allowed themselves

to be 'haunted by a fear of historicism' long after this had ceased to be a threat as well as allowing their judgement to be impaired by an anxiety to be taken for scientists, albeit social scientists.

12 p. 441.

13 *The Evolution of Culture and Other Essays*, ed. J.L. Myres (Oxford 1906), 53.

14 W.J. Sollas, *Ancient Hunters*, 3rd edn (London 1926), 131–2.

15 V. Gordon Childe, 'Changing methods and aims in prehistory. Presidential Address for 1935', *Proc. Prehist. Soc.* I (1935), 1–15.

16 D.A.E. Garrod, '*Nova et Vetera*: a plea for a new method in Palaeolithic research. Presidential Address for 1928', *Proc. Prehist. Soc. East Anglia* V, 260–72; 'The Upper Palaeolithic in the light of recent discovery', *Proc. Prehist. Soc.* IV (1938), 1–26.

17 As in the Rhind Lectures for 1945. These appeared as *Scotland before the Scots* (London 1946).

18 *Man Makes Himself*, op.cit., 238.

19 'Valediction', *Bull. Inst. Archaeol.*, no. I (1958), 1–8.

20 cf. V.G. Childe, *What Happened in History* (London 1942), chap. 12.

21 V.G. Childe, *Social Evolution* (London 1951), 163 ff.

22 *Prehistoric Times*, 4th edn (1878), 607 f.

23 *Man Makes Himself*, 4th edn (London 1966), 235.

24 Grahame Clark, *Mesolithic Prelude* (Edinburgh 1980), *passim*.

Chapter 4. The genesis of cultural diversity

1 E. Cassirer, *An Essay on Man* (New Haven 1962), 228.

2 Quoted from p. xviii of vol. I of *The Bradenham Edition of the Novels and Tales of Benjamin Disraeli* (London 1926).

3 G. Clark, 'Domestication and social evolution', *Phil. Trans. Roy. Soc. Lond. B.* 275, no. 936 (1976), 5–11.

4 J. Desmond Clark, *The Prehistory of Africa* (London 1970), 103; also in G. Isaac and E.R. McCown (eds), *Human Evolution: Louis Leakey and the East African Experience* (Menlo Park, Calif. 1976), 45.

5 J. Desmond Clark, op.cit., 103 f.

6 G. Clark, *World Prehistory in New Perspective* (Cambridge 1977), 353.

7 C.B.M. McBurney, *Early Man in the Soviet Union. The Implications*

of Some Recent Discoveries, Reckitt Lecture, British Academy (1976).

8 O.P. Chernish, *The Palaeolithic site Molodova V* (Kiev 1961).

9 G. Clark, *World Prehistory*, 321 ff.

10 ibid., 353.

11 ibid., 352–61.

12 ibid., fig. 205.

13 P.J. Ucko and G.W. Dimbleby (eds), *The Domestication and Exploitation of Plants and Animals* (London 1969); Sir Joseph Hutchinson *et al.* (eds), 'The Early History of Agriculture', *Phil. Trans. Roy. Soc. Lond.* B. 275, no. 936 (1976), 1–213; G. Clark, *Mesolithic Prelude* (Edinburgh 1980), 9–15.

14 Elman Service, *Primitive Social Organisation* (New York 1962), 144.

15 T.G.E. Powell, *Prehistoric Art* (London 1966), chap. iv, 'The art of a barbarian nation'; Paul Jacobsthal, *Early Celtic Art*, 2 vols (Oxford 1969); J.V.S. Megaw, *Art of the European Iron Age* (Bath 1970); John Brailsford, *Early Celtic Masterpieces from Britain* (London 1978).

16 R.A. Smith, *A Guide to the Anglo-Saxon and Foreign Teutonic Antiquities* (London 1923); T.D. Kendrick, *Anglo-Saxon Art to AD 900* (London 1938); R. Jessup, *Anglo-Saxon Jewellery* (London 1950); R. Bruce-Mitford, *The Sutton Hoo Ship-burial. A Handbook*, 2nd edn (London 1972); *The Sutton Hoo Ship-burial*, vol. 2: *Arms, Armour and Regalia* (London 1978).

Chapter 5. The findings of ethnography

1 A.M. Lysaght, 'Banks' artists and his *Endeavour* collections', in T.C. Mitchell (ed.), *Captain Cook and the South Pacific* (London 1979), 9–80.

2 Reproduced on figs. 51 and 98 of Hugh Cobb (ed.), *Cook's Voyages and Peoples of the Pacific* (London 1979).

3 The originals are now in the Peabody Museum at Harvard. Examples have recently been reproduced in: *Cook's Voyages and Peoples of the Pacific*, fig. 74; Philip Drucker, *Cultures of the North Pacific Coast* (San Francisco 1965), 146–7; and Grahame Clark, *World Prehistory*, 3rd edn (Cambridge 1977), fig. 223.

4 Alan Moorehead, *Darwin and the Beagle* (Harmondsworth 1971).

5 John Oxley, *Journals of Two Expeditions into the Interior of New South Wales* (London 1820); see also G. Clark, op.cit., fig. 287.

6 Donald F. Thomson, 'The seasonal factor in human culture', *Proc.*

Prehist. Soc. (1939), 200–1, and 'Some wood and stone implements of the Bindibu Tribe of Central Western Australia', ibid. (1964), 400–22.

7 Richard A. Gould, *Yiwara: Foragers of the Australian Desert* (London 1969).

8 Adrienne L. Kaeppler, 'Tracing the history of the Hawaiian Cook Voyage Artefacts in the Museum of Mankind', in *Captain Cook and the South Pacific*, 167–97.

9 For illustrations of leading specimens see J.C.H. King, 'The Nootka of Vancouver Island', *Cook's Voyages and Peoples of the Pacific*, 89–108.

10 Wilfred Shawcross, 'The Cambridge University collection of Maori artefacts, made on Captain Cook's first voyage', *J. Polynesian Soc.* 79 (1970), 305–48.

11 C. Daryll Forde, *Habitat, Economy and Society. A Geographical Introduction to Ethnology* (London 1934), chap. VIII.

12 Therkel Mathiassen, *Material Culture of the Iglulik Eskimos*, Report of the 5th Thule Expedition 1921–4 (Copenhagen 1942), especially chaps VII–VIII.

13 op.cit., 3.

14 Thomson, 'The seasonal factor in human culture' op. cit. 1939.

15 E.E. Evans-Pritchard, *The Nuer. A Description of the Modes of Livelihood and Political Institutions of a Nilotic People* (Oxford 1940).

16 W.W. Fitzhugh, *Environmental Archaeology and Cultural Systems in Hamilton Inlet, Labrador*, Smithsonian Contributions to Anthropology no. 16 (Washington 1972).

17 Richard B. Lee, 'Kung Bushman subsistence: an input-output analysis', in A.P. Vayda (ed.), *Environment and Cultural Behaviour* (New York 1969), 47–79.

18 P. Nørlund, *Viking Settlers in Greenland* (Cambridge 1936).

19 A.H. Quiggin, 'Costume and adornment, primitive', *Chambers's Encyclopaedia*, new edn (London 1950), vol. 4, 167a.

20 Particularly impressive work has been done on the recording, display and conservation of peasant costume in Scandinavia and the Balkans. The Nordiska Museet and its associated folk museum at Skansen, both in Stockholm, are outstanding. For Danish costume, see Ellen Andersen, *Folkedragter i Nationalmuseet* (Copenhagen 1971). An outstanding display of central European folk costume and associated arts may be seen in the Slovak museum at Martin.

21 'Primitive Art', *The Listener* XXV (1941), 598–9.

22 *Elements of Social Organisation* (London 1951), chap. V.

23 London 1965.

24 *Kinship and the Social Order* (Chicago 1969), 13.

25 Op.cit., 104.

26 ibid., 128.

27 Erik Holm, 'The rock-art of South Africa', in H.G. Bandi (ed.), *The Art of the Stone Age* (New York 1961), 153–203; see also Carleton Coon's review in *Science* 142 (1963), 1644.

28 S.G. Morley, *The Ancient Maya*, 3rd edn, rev. by George W. Brainerd (Stanford 1956); Michael D. Coe, *The Maya* (London 1971), chap. 8.

29 Cyril Aldred, *Egypt to the End of the Old Kingdom* (London 1965), 51.

30 J. Gernet, *Daily Life in China on the Eve of the Mongol Invasion. 1250–1276* (London 1962).

31 Edmund Leach, *Political Systems of Highland Burma* (London 1954), 5. The effectiveness of Leach's attack is apparent from the defensive tone of Max Gluckman's 'The utility of the equilibrium model in the study of social change', *Amer. Anthrop.* 70 (1968), 219–37.

32 Thorstein Veblen, *The Theory of the Leisure Class* (New York 1899).

33 Peter Bellwood, *Man's Conquest of the Pacific* (London 1979).

34 Raymond Firth, *Economics of the New Zealand Maori* (Wellington 1959).

Chapter 6. High culture in hierarchical societies

1 In P.R.S. Moorey (ed.), *The Origins of Civilization* (Oxford 1979), 19 ff.

2 S. Zuckerman, *The Social Life of Monkeys and Apes* (London 1932), 233–4.

3 E.g. V.C. Wynne-Edwards, *Animal Dispersal in Relation to Social Behaviour* (Edinburgh 1962), 138–44; and K.R.L. Hall, 'Social organisation of the Old World monkeys and apes', *Symposium of the Zoological Society of London*, 14 (1965), 265–89, and in Phyllis C. Jay (ed.), *Primate Studies in Adaptation and Variability* (New York 1968), 7–31.

4 Wynne-Edwards, op.cit., 143–4.

5 Konrad Lorenz, *On Aggression* (London 1966), 35 f.

6 L. Pales, 'Les Neandertaliens en France', in G.H.R. von Koenigswald (ed.), *Hundert Jahre Neanderthaler* (Cologne 1958), 35.

7 R.M. Yerkes, *Chimpanzees: A Laboratory Colony* (New Haven, 1943).

8 M. Yamada, 'A case of acculturation in a subhuman society of Japanese monkeys', *Primates* I (1957), 30–46.

9 A. Irving Hallowell, *Social Life of Early Man*, ed. S.L. Washburn (London 1962), 247.

10 D. Diringer, *Writing* (London 1962).

11 Henri Frankfort, *The Birth of Civilization in the Near East* (London 1951), 16.

12 Further references will be found in the following introductory works: Cyril Aldred, *Egypt to the end of the Old Kingdom* (London 1965); T.G.H. James, *An Introduction to Ancient Egypt* (London 1979).

13 James, ibid., 155.

14 I.E.S. Edwards, *The Pyramids of Egypt* (Harmondsworth 1975).

15 Edward Chiera, *They Wrote on Clay* (Chicago 1938); Frankfort, op.cit., chap. III; Max Mallowan, *Early Mesopotamia and Iran* (London 1965); D. and J. Oates, *The Rise of Civilisation* (London 1976).

16 C.L. Woolley, *Ur Excavations: II, The Royal Cemetery* (London 1934); *Excavations at Ur: a Record of Twelve Years' Work* (London 1954).

17 A. Leo Oppenheim, *Ancient Mesopotamia* (Chicago 1964).

18 J. Ayres and J. Rawson, *Chinese Jade through the Ages* (London 1975); Chang Kwang-chih, *The Archaeology of Ancient China* (London 1977); John K. Fairbank (ed.), *Chinese Thought and Institutions* (Chicago 1957); Li Chi, *The Beginnings of Chinese Civilization* (Seattle 1957); Jessica Rawson, *Ancient China. Art and Archaeology* (London 1980); Michael Sullivan, *A Short History of Chinese Art* (London 1967); W. Watson, *Ancient Chinese Bronzes* (London 1962); W. Willets, *Foundations of Chinese Art* (London 1965).

19 op. cit., 63.

20 ibid., 195.

21 T'ung-Tsu Ch'u, 'Chinese class structure and its ideology', in J.K. Fairbank (ed.), op.cit., 235–50.

22 Hsiao-Tung Fei, *China's Gentry. Essays in Rural-Urban Relations*, ed. M.P. Redfield (Chicago 1953), 97.

23 *Renoir, My Father* (London 1962), 387 ff.

Chapter 7. Homogenization and dehumanization

1 John Paul II, *John Paul II in Mexico: His Collected Speeches* (London 1979), 74 f.; Edward Norman, 'The moral and political attitudes of Pope John Paul II', *The Cambridge Review* I (June 1981), 194–202.

2 José Ortega y Gasset, *The Dehumanization of Art and other essays* (Princeton 1968), 191.

3 George P. Adams, *The Idea of Civilization*, Symposium (Berkeley 1941), 51.

4 Clifford Geertz, *The Interpretation of Cultures. Selected Essays* (New York 1973), 52.

5 As in his *Mass Civilization and Minority Culture* (1930) or in the book he wrote with Denys Thompson, *Culture and Environment* (1933) in which he stressed the effects of mass-production and standardization.

6 *Bulletin of the American Academy of Arts and Sciences* xxxv (1981), 4–23.

7 Grahame Clark, *World Prehistory and Natural Science*, Det Kongelige Danske Videnskab. Selsk. Hist.-Fil. Kl. 50:I (Copenhagen 1980).

8 Jean Renoir, *Renoir, My Father* (London 1962).

9 Herbert Read, *Art and the Evolution of Man* (London 1951), 12.

10 Much of the text of pp. 154–8 is reprinted by permission from my essay 'Archaeology and Human Diversity', *Ann. Rev. Anthrop.* (1979), 1–20.

11 Karl Popper, *The Open Society and its Enemies*, 5th edn (London 1966), vol. I, 70.

12 ibid., 200.

13 T.R. Berger, 'Mining and exploration effects: the Canadian experience . . .', *Australian Inst. of Aboriginal Studies Newsletter* (Canberra), no. 12 (September 1979), 9–24.

14 Axel Steensberg, *Report of a Mission to Australia, New Zealand and New Guinea (1970–1)*, privately printed (Copenhagen 1972), 6.

15 R. Dahrendorf, *Essays in the Theory of Society* (Stanford 1968), 151–78.

16 *Historical Relics unearthed in New China* (Peking 1972).

17 Renoir, op.cit., 209.

18 Dahrendorf, op.cit., 42.

Index